THE
LITTLE
HISTORY
OF
SOMERSET

THE
LITTLE
HISTORY

OF

SOMERSET

MIKE DEAN

First published 2020

The History Press
97 St George's Place, Cheltenham,
Gloucestershire, GL50 3QB
www.thehistorypress.co.uk

British Library Cataloguing in Publication Data.
A catalogue record for this book is available from the British Library.

ISBN 978 0 7509 9127 8

Typesetting and origination by The History Press
Printed in Turkey by Imak.

CONTENTS

ABOUT THE AUTHOR

Mike Dean is a retired primary school teacher and a registered Blue Badge Tour Guide for the West of England. A graduate of Bristol University, his hobbies include reading, walking, music and travel. He is a West Countryman by birth, with a lifelong interest in the history and traditions of the area. His first book, *A Little Book of Bath*, is published by The History Press. He lives in Keynsham, between Bristol and Bath.

ACKNOWLEDGEMENTS

I would like to express my thanks to a number of people, without whose help this book could not have been written. The staff of the public libraries of Keynsham, Bath and Glastonbury have been helpful in locating books and other sources of information, and I am also grateful to City Archivist Colin Johnston and his colleagues at Bath Record Office. Also (and not least) to my wife, Gwyneth, for her encouragement and support, as well as for some helpful suggestions.

INTRODUCTION

This book is not intended to be an exhaustive or scholarly tome on the history of Somerset. For anyone wishing to study this fascinating and rewarding county in depth, there are several very comprehensive studies that will enable them to do so, and some of these are listed at the end of this book. My aim here has been to provide a general overview of Somerset's history from earliest times to the present, in an accessible, readable and (I hope) interesting form. I have tried to cover all the major events, as well as some of the less well-known (but nonetheless important) ones. I've also included a few stories and anecdotes that I think help to bring the past to life.

To get to know an area it helps enormously if you know something of its past, and how it came to be the way it is. I hope that this book will help to increase the enjoyment and understanding of those visiting, or passing through, Somerset, as well, perhaps, as some who live here but maybe do not know their county as well as they would like. If it does this, it will have achieved what it set out to do.

1

THE BEGINNINGS OF SOMERSET

THE GROUND BENEATH YOUR FEET

Imagine yourself, about 200 million years ago, standing on the edge of a piece of land roughly where Swindon now stands and looking south-westwards. In front of you lies a large expanse of water, with, here and there, what appears to be a low-lying island sticking up above the surface. What you are looking at will one day be the West Country, and the part nearest to you will be Somerset.

The oldest rocks in Somerset were formed at an even earlier time – more than 400 million years ago. If you look at a geological map of the county you will see that most of its underlying rocks are of the sedimentary kind, such as limestone, sandstone, marl, lias and clay. The sediments of which these rocks are composed were deposited on the seabed during the period, millions of years ago, when what is now the south-western part of Britain was covered by warm, shallow seas. Under pressure, these deposits solidified and became rocks, which later seismic disturbances folded and pushed above the surface of the sea, where they gradually became land. This folding produced the ranges of hills that are such a feature of the county: the Mendips, Quantocks, Poldens and Blackdowns. These sedimentary rocks, because they were not subjected to intense heat, can often contain fossils of the plant and animal life that existed on earth long before the coming of humans. As recently as 2018, a jawbone found on a beach at Lilstock in Bridgwater Bay has been identified as that of a giant ichthyosaur, a creature that lived around 200 million years ago and was almost as large as a blue whale.

The outcome of all this geological upheaval is a county that has a great variety of scenery. It has a coastline that stretches from Avonmouth in the north-east to Sugarloaf Hill in the south-west, a distance of approximately 71 miles (115km) (this refers to the traditional county of Somerset, of which more later). Inland there are moors, hills and valleys, together with wetlands, woodlands and farmland, and the highest inland cliffs in the United Kingdom. The soft limestone rocks contain numerous cave systems and there are also extensive coal measures, laid down during the Carboniferous period (about 300 million years ago). These were created from dead plant matter, overlaid with rock and converted by heat and pressure into carbon deposits. All of these factors have contributed to Somerset's fascinating history, and form the 'bones' of the county.

In the Mendip area, many of the limestone caves were blocked with permafrost during successive Ice Ages, making the limestone temporarily impermeable. Then, when the ice melted, the water was forced to the surface, where it carved out natural features such as the dramatic Cheddar Gorge, with its 500ft (140m) cliffs.

But what about the people?

THE EARLIEST HUMANS

The first evidence we have of human habitation in the area, in the form of flint tools and other artefacts, shows that people may have been living here as long as half a million years ago. These early humans, known as *Homo Erectus*, were probably ancestors of the Neanderthals, and occupied caves in places such as Cheddar and Burrington, where artefacts such as stone hand axes have been discovered (see illustration). Excavations at a quarry above Westbury-sub-Mendip have produced evidence of some of the earliest human habitation in Britain. These people were hunter-gatherers, foraging for food and hunting animals and birds for survival. Bison, reindeer, bears and smaller animals are known to have roamed the area, providing food, clothing and even primitive tools for these early communities. In Burrington Combe, not far from Cheddar, is a cave known as Aveline's Hole. Here, in 1797, two men digging for a rabbit discovered a number of skeletons that were dated at more than 10,000 years old, making this the earliest known cemetery in Britain.

About 10,000 years ago, at the end of the last Ice Age, forests covered much of the area, except for the higher hills. With the melting of the ice the subsequent rise in sea level caused much of the present Somerset Levels to become waterlogged, creating mudflats and marshes where fish and waterfowl were abundant (even today, some parts of Somerset are below present sea level). From this period comes Cheddar Man, who is sometimes regarded as the first 'modern' Briton, and whose skeleton is the oldest complete one to have been found in Britain. It was discovered in Gough's Cave, Cheddar, in 1903. Damage to the skull suggests that he probably died by violence. Interestingly, recent DNA analysis from the skeleton has thrown up two matches with people living in the village of Cheddar today. It also tells us that these distant ancestors of ours probably had dark skin, blue eyes and dark curly hair.

Britain became an island about 8,000 years ago, when a further rise in sea level separated us from the rest of Europe. By about 4,500 BC a new wave of people from the Continent had moved into Britain. These Neolithic (or New Stone Age) folk, as we now call them, brought new ideas with them. They were farmers and stockbreeders, growing crops and raising animals in settled communities. They have left us tantalising clues about the way they lived and died, including their burial mounds, standing stones and stone circles, such as the one at Stanton Drew. Archaeologists are still not in complete agreement over the reasons for these stone circles, although it's thought

they were most likely constructed for religious or ritual purposes. These people also produced pottery and other artefacts, and, in Somerset, built wooden trackways to cross the marshy areas, one of which, known as the Sweet Track, dates from about 4,000 BC. It is about 2km in length and is believed to be one of the oldest in Europe. Signs of human activity have been found in places such as South Cadbury, and some caves in the Mendip Hills have shown evidence of occupation at that time.

The people of the late Neolithic and early Bronze Age period produced a distinctive type of pottery used as drinking vessels, which has led to them being known as the 'Beaker Folk'. The dead would usually be buried in pits, but more important individuals would be interred in long barrows, made of earth and containing wood- or stone-lined chambers, where bones or cremated remains would be deposited. A good example of a long barrow can be seen at Stoney Littleton, near the village of Wellow.

BRONZE AGE SOMERSET (ABOUT 2,500 BC–800 BC)

By the middle of the Bronze Age, 'villages' of stone huts with conical thatched roofs were being built, surrounded by a low wall. This more settled existence meant that the villagers had the time and leisure to produce much more elaborate artefacts, and, as the name suggests, they were workers in bronze, which is an alloy of copper and tin, and produced not only weapons but also ornaments, which they could trade with other communities. They also began to divide the landscape around them into small square or rectangular fields separated by low stone banks, traces of which can still be found on Exmoor. Plant and insect evidence tells us that temperatures in this period were, on average, 2–4 degrees cooler in winter and 2–3 degrees warmer in summer than today, which determined what crops they could grow (mostly wheat, barley, oats and pulses). In Somerset, evidence of these Bronze Age settlements has been found at such locations as South Cadbury, Brean Down and on Exmoor.

The dead were buried in smaller, round barrows, sometimes grouped together, as at Priddy Nine Barrows on the Mendips, and there are many other examples on Exmoor, such as Alderman's Barrow near Exford.

IRON AGE SOMERSET (ABOUT 800 BC–AD 43)

This period saw a significant increase in population and, consequently, a greater demand on available resources. Iron, being harder and more durable, was replacing bronze as the principal material for making weapons and tools. Communities became more territorial, and we see the increasing construction of hill forts, such as those at

Brent Knoll, Maesbury and Cadbury Castle. These were constructed on easily defensible positions, with good views all around, and defended by banks and ditches. Some of them were massive constructions that would have needed huge numbers of people to build them, and years to construct. The largest in the county (and one of the largest in Britain) is Ham Hill near Yeovil, which covers an area of 210 acres (85ha) and is 400ft (122m) high. Altogether there are about forty-seven of these hill forts in Somerset, most having been built during the fifth and sixth centuries BC. Hill forts are also known to have been part of a network of trade and exchange. Excavations at sites such as Cadbury Castle have unearthed examples of pottery from Devon and Cornwall and even amber from the Baltic. Late Iron Age smiths were producing beautiful and elaborate bronze and gold objects, which were often buried with important community leaders.

These Iron Age people are also known as 'Celts' (the origin of the name is unclear, but might have its origin in Greek, and mean 'the tall ones'). The three main tribes occupying Somerset during this period were the Durotriges (who occupied the south of the county) the Dobunni in the north, and the Dumnonii in the west. They had a shared culture and seem to have co-existed more or less amicably. According to the Roman Solinus, writing in the third century AD, the Dumnonii did not use coins – none have been found during excavations – preferring to use barter as a means of trading. They would most likely have traded with the Silures of South Wales, who are known to have used the same system. The main religious site was at present-day Bath, where the hot springs were regarded as sacred and under the protection of a deity named Sulis (more will be said about this later, when we deal with the Roman period).

In the low-lying area known today as the Somerset Levels, lake villages were built, the most important being at Glastonbury and Meare. These were built on artificial 'islands' and consisted of circular houses with thatched roofs and walls of wattle and daub (this consists of woven branches plastered with a sticky material, usually containing clay, sand, straw and sometimes animal dung). The Glastonbury village had about fifteen houses and a population of around 200, and, being surrounded by water, was easy to defend. However, rising water levels eventually forced the abandonment of these villages, but excavations during the late nineteenth century revealed much evidence, including the remains of a dugout log boat. This, along with many other finds, is on display in the Lake Village Museum in Glastonbury High Street.

The remains of one of the largest Iron Age 'roundhouses' in Britain was discovered in 2009, during excavations at the location of a proposed 'Park and Ride' site at Taunton. These dwellings were similar in design to the Bronze Age huts, but tended to be larger, and the walls were made of upright timbers filled with wattle and daub, like the lake village houses.

THE ROMANS (WHAT DID THEY EVER DO FOR SOMERSET?)

Following the invasion carried out under the emperor Claudius in AD 43, the legions moved westwards, soon reaching what we now call Somerset. The fact that they encountered some pretty stiff resistance while bringing the area under their control can be guessed by the finding of early Roman military equipment at the sites of some of the hill forts, particularly Ham Hill. Here, pieces of armour, spear heads and ballista bolts have been unearthed (the ballista was a kind of giant crossbow). Cadbury Castle was also the scene of some fierce action, most likely against the second Augusta Legion under the command of Vespasian in about AD 60.

It is likely that some of the local tribes in Somerset were already trading with the Romans before the Claudian invasion, and some were quick to adopt the Roman lifestyle. The newcomers brought many innovations with them; they introduced vineyards (modern versions of which are enjoying considerable success in Somerset) and cereals such as spelt (also making a comeback). Apples, of the kind we are familiar with today, plums, pears, cucumber, carrots and many other crops were almost certainly brought here by the Romans. They established a number of towns in the West of England, including in Somerset. A particular attraction of this county was the presence of lead and silver in the area of the Mendip Hills, and the Romans mined these extensively in the locality of Charterhouse, where the remains of their workings can still be seen. A Roman lead 'pig' has been found in France, and it is thought that Mendip lead was probably used in the building of Rome's Colosseum.

The Romans also established a number of rural sites in Somerset, most of them villas, or country estates, such as the one discovered in 1887 during the construction of the Somerset and Dorset Railway. The two most significant settlements in the county are those of Ilchester and Bath. At Ilchester, which the Romans called Lindinis, they first established a timber fort, or *castra*, and this was gradually developed into a stone-walled town that seems to have consisted mostly of private houses for wealthy owners.

Christianity had, of course, found its way into Britain before the coming of the Romans, but when, early in the fourth century, it became accepted within the Roman Empire, its influence began to spread more widely, although many still worshipped the old pagan gods. At the romantically named Pagan's Hill, near Chew Stoke, the remains of a Romano–British temple were excavated in the early 1950s. The temple dated from the early third century and was probably dedicated to the Roman god Mercury. Somerset is also comparatively rich in Romano–British cemeteries, such as the one near Shepton Mallet, and villa sites, such as Dinnington, near Crewkerne, which was probably occupied by Christianised Romano–Britons.

But what did they sound like? As far as we can gather, the native language spoken in the area during this period was what is now called Southwestern Brythonic. This is a Celtic tongue, very similar to Cornish and Welsh (into which it eventually evolved), as well as old Breton. However, very little written evidence of this language remains, apart from a few inscribed stones and possibly a few of the 'curse tablets' found in excavations at Bath. Traces also survive in some words we still use today, especially those describing natural features, such as 'coombe' (*cwm*) – a valley, Avon (*afon*) – a river and 'tor' (*twrr*) – a lofty hill.

BATH LIKE A ROMAN

Easily the most important settlement in Somerset was at present-day Bath, where the presence of the only natural hot springs in Britain encouraged the Romans to settle and to establish a town that centred on the great baths complex. From about AD 80 until the early fifth century, Bath became famous throughout the Roman Empire as a social, religious and health spa resort. The temple built here was dedicated to Minerva, the Roman goddess of healing and wisdom, but the Celtic tribe who preceded the Romans in the area had believed the guardian of the waters to be a deity named Sul, or Sulis, so the Roman settlers simply linked the two deities together and named their town Aquae Sulis (the waters of Sulis). Although not large (the town was only about 23 acres [9.3ha] in extent) it attracted visitors in great numbers, and the local population gradually adapted to the Roman way of life.

When Roman occupation ended, the baths complex fell into ruin and was gradually built over. The Roman baths themselves were rediscovered in the late nineteenth century, and subsequent excavations have uncovered thousands of artefacts that give a fascinating insight into the lives of the Romano–British folk who lived and worked here. Burials were not permitted within the town walls, but many tombstones have been discovered outside the town that give a good idea of the community that once occupied the town. They range from a stone commemorating Successa Petronia, a 3-year-old girl, to one for an 80-year-old senator from Glevum (Gloucester).

Many offerings to the goddess were thrown into the sacred spring, as well as curses, inscribed on lead and sometimes written backwards (so that only a god would understand!). These were mostly requests for the goddess to punish someone who had wronged the donor in some way, such as theft. In the temple courtyard animals would be sacrificed on a stone altar, then their entrails would be inspected by the *haruspex* (or augurer) to try to determine what the future held. A messy business!

ROMAN ROADS

The Fosse Way

The great Roman road known as the Fosse Way ran from Exeter (Isca Dumnoniorum) in the south-west to Lincoln (Lindum) in the north-east, and for part of its 230-mile (370km) length it ran through Somerset. It was constructed in the mid-first century AD, probably for military purposes, and the name 'fosse' comes from the Latin 'fossa', meaning a ditch, after the defensive ditch that marked the western boundary of Roman-controlled Britain. Many miles of the modern A367 and the A37 roads in Somerset follow the line of the Fosse Way. For the construction of the road through Somerset the builders used the local Ham stone, the honey-coloured material that was later used for decorative carvings on many a Somerset church.

The Via Julia

Between Bristol and the mouth of the River Avon lies the settlement of Sea Mills, known in Roman times as 'Abona' or 'Portus Abonae'. This was a small Roman port, which probably had links with the Roman town of Caerleon, on the other side of the Bristol Channel and almost opposite the mouth of the river. From Abona, a Roman road, believed to have been named the 'Via Julia', extended eastwards and linked with the important Roman spa town of Aquae Sulis (Bath).

FAKE OR FORTUNE?

In 1990, during excavations near Shepton Mallet for the building of a new warehouse, a small Roman cemetery was uncovered, and an amulet found. This bore the 'Chi-Rho' monogram (an early Christian symbol representing the first two letters of Christ's name in Greek), and was thought to be one of the earliest examples of a Christian artefact discovered in Britain. A copy was presented to the then Archbishop of Canterbury, but subsequent tests revealed the original to be almost certainly a hoax, possibly planted in an attempt to halt the construction of the warehouse (which was built anyway)!

Other finds have proved to be genuine. In April 2010 one of the largest hoards of Roman coins ever discovered in Britain was unearthed by means of a metal detector near Frome. Known as the 'Frome Hoard', it consisted of more than 52,000 coins dating from the third century AD. They have been valued at around £320,000.

THE SAXONS ARRIVE

After the end of Roman occupation in the early fifth century, the next wave of invaders was the Saxons, who came across the North Sea. They were a mix of people from Denmark, Holland and Germany. The name 'Saxon' probably derives from the 'seax', a kind of long knife or short sword favoured by their warriors (its name is still preserved in the counties of Essex and Sussex). As with the Romans before them, the Saxon culture and influence spread westwards, so that much of the West Country, including Somerset, became known as 'Wessex', the kingdom of the West Saxons. The spread and settlement of the Saxons was not always peaceful. The *Anglo–Saxon Chronicle* (begun in the ninth century) tells us that in AD 577 a great battle was fought at Deorham (Dyrham) in Gloucestershire, in which two Saxon chieftains, Cuthwine and Ceawlin, 'slew three English kings' and captured three towns, including Bath (or Bathanceaster, as it is called in the *Chronicle*).

To add to the troubles of the native Britons in Somerset, in 658 Cenwalh, the Saxon King of Wessex, invaded Somerset, and following the Battle of Peonnum, took control of the county as far west as the River Parrett. 'Peonnum' might have been Penselwood near Wincanton, or possibly Penn, near Yeovil.

We know from early records that the old Celtic place names were sometimes changed by the Saxon newcomers. For example, Biddisham, near Axbridge, had formerly been *Tarnuc,* and the Celtic settlement of *Lantokai,* near Glastonbury, had its name changed to the much more down-to-earth Leigh.

In the eighth and ninth centuries Somerset had no towns as we would recognise them. Royal centres, such as the one at Cheddar, would probably have just the palace and a few associated buildings. Such activities as trade and manufacture, which today we would associate with towns, would take place either here or in the monasteries. A typical Saxon palace would need to be of a sufficient size to accommodate the king and all his followers. It would be constructed of wood and might have two floors, the lower floor consisting of a long hall running the length of the building. Around this would be grouped stables, barns, storehouses, workshops and lodgings. Somerset would have had several of these royal palaces, although Cheddar is the only site so far where such a building has been positively identified.

Lower down the social ladder, a charter of 963 relates to a Saxon estate called Manworthy, near Milverton, and refers to a 'hollow ditch', or 'hollow way'. These were ditches dug by each landowner to mark the boundaries of his property.

KING INE

One of the most notable of the early Saxon kings of Wessex was Ine, who reigned between 688 and 726. According to some sources he was born in Somerton, and his aim as king was to extend the area of his influence, particularly westwards into the territory of the Dumnonii. In 710 he defeated Geraint, King of Dumnonia, in battle, thereby extending his territory into Devon as far as the River Tamar. He then built a new fortress at Taunton, but in 722, according to the *Anglo–Saxon Chronicle*, this was destroyed by Ine's wife, Queen Aethelburg (or Ethelburga), apparently to deny it to the enemy forces of Ealdbert, a rival chieftain who was eventually killed by Ine. After this, Ine abdicated and went with his wife to Rome, where he died.

'KING' ARTHUR

The opposition of the native Britons to the invading Saxons is commemorated in the legends that surround Arthur, who was most likely a local chieftain who led the resistance in the west. His headquarters may well have been at the hill fort of South Cadbury, referred to earlier. His determined resistance, culminating in a great battle at 'Mount Badon' (possibly Solsbury Hill near Bath), was so successful that the invaders were driven back to occupy only a relatively small area of the country. Arthur's struggles were also seen as defending the Christian faith against the pagan invaders. His heroic deeds were later romanticised and developed into the mythical tales of King Arthur, together with his knights, Camelot, the sword Excalibur and the Round Table. Glastonbury, otherwise Avalon, has become, in legend, the burial place of Arthur and his Queen, Guinevere.

The boundary between Wessex and its neighbour Mercia was roughly defined by the rivers Avon and Thames. Aethelbald, King of Mercia, was keen to extend his authority into Wessex, and the *Anglo–Saxon Chronicle* tells us that 'in 733, Aethelbald overcame Somerton. The sun darkened.' Somerton, at that time, was probably the capital of Wessex, and this entry in the *Chronicle* is the earliest reference to it.

'THE FURY OF THE NORTHMEN'

During the ninth and tenth centuries the coastal areas in many parts of England were plagued by attacks by warriors from the Scandinavian countries of Norway, Denmark and Sweden. These warriors, known as 'Vikings' (the name is more of a job description than a nationality) came to grab plunder wherever they could find it. The first recorded instance of a Viking attack on Somerset was in 854, when, as the *Anglo–Saxon Chronicle* tells us, 'the men of Somerset ... with the men of Dorset, fought at the mouth of the River Parret with a Danish army there (and) made great slaughter'.

In 878 a force of Vikings, under the leadership of Ubba Ragnarsson, came ashore and laid siege to a fort known as 'Cynuit'. One location that has been suggested for this is Combwich, on the River Parret near Bridgwater. The Vikings numbered 23 ships and about 1,200 men. They were opposed by a force led by Odda, an ealdorman (or local leader appointed by the king) of Devon, and the Norsemen were defeated. They lost their cherished raven banner (said to have been woven by Ubba's three sisters) in the conflict, and Ubba himself was killed.

HOW 'GREAT' WAS ALFRED?

Alfred (reigned 871–899) is the only British monarch to be known as 'the Great'. Born in 849 in Wantage (now in Oxfordshire), he succeeded his brother Aethelred as King of Wessex in 871, and spent several years fighting against Danish Viking invaders. After a disastrous defeat at Chippenham, Wiltshire, in 878, Alfred was forced to retreat into the low-lying marshes of Somerset, where he made a fort at Athelney. From this period comes the famous legend of his sheltering in a peasant woman's cottage, and being scolded by her when he allowed the cakes to burn that she had asked him to watch (not knowing, of course, who he was). From Athelney, supported by the local Somerset fyrd, or militia, he mounted a strong counterattack, which concluded with a decisive victory over the Danes at the Battle of Edington, Wiltshire, in the same year. A peace treaty was then signed at Wedmore, Somerset, under the terms of which Guthrum, the Viking leader, converted to Christianity and accepted Alfred as his adoptive father. To protect against further raids, Alfred had *burghs*, or fortified towns, built throughout his kingdom (this is where the modern word 'borough' comes from). Taunton, Wells and Bridgwater were formerly Saxon burghs. During Alfred's reign a Saxon palace was built at Cheddar, with a wooden 'great hall'. This was later enlarged and became a royal hunting lodge. During the tenth century the 'Witan', or *Witenagemot*, was held here several times. This was an assembly of the ruling class, comprising the most important noblemen in England, both lay and ecclesiastical, at which their task was to advise the king. The remains of the palace were excavated during the building of the Kings of Wessex School in 1963, and the site is now marked with concrete.

As a king, Alfred was a man of great piety and considerable learning, both of which he was anxious to encourage among his subjects. He tried his hand at ship design, and had a small fleet of warships built that were twice the size of the Viking longships. These were to prove successful in dealing with future raids. He also had a *'herepath'*, or military road, constructed, which led westwards across the Quantocks and allowed fast movement of troops.

In 1693 the ornament that has become known as 'the Alfred Jewel' was discovered in Somerset. It is made of gold and crystal, and bears the inscription '*AELFRED MEC HEHT GEWYRCAN*' ('Alfred had me made'). It's thought that it might once have formed part of a pointer used when reading a religious text. Today it can be seen in the Ashmolean Museum in Oxford.

If Somerset thought it had seen the last of the Vikings, however, it was mistaken, because in 914 raiding parties landed at Watchet and at Porlock, but were beaten off with heavy losses. The survivors had to swim for it, and spent some time on the island of Steep Holm in the Bristol Channel, from which they carried out sporadic raids on Watchet and Porlock. After that, the Vikings seem mostly to have left Somerset alone until renewed Danish attacks under King Swein Forkbeard in 1013 resulted in a truce at Bath in which the western *thegns* (noblemen) submitted to him. A Viking sword found in the city ditch in Bath in the late twentieth century may date from this occasion.

THE 'UNREADY' KING

King Aethelred II (r. 978–1013 and 1014–16) is sometimes known as 'the Unready' because of his Saxon nickname 'Unraed', but the word really means 'badly advised'. He conceived the idea of trying to buy off the Danes by paying them protection money, known as 'Danegeld', and a number of these coins still exist in Scandinavian museums. These museums contain examples of coins from the Somerset towns of Axbridge, Bath, Crewkerne, Ilchester, Taunton and Watchet, all of which, like many other English towns, had their own mint. Not all of these coins were necessarily part of the Danegeld, but it is likely that some were. As with all protection rackets, the recipients kept coming back for more!

WHAT'S IN A NAME?

During the Saxon period England began to be divided into 'shires' for the purposes of local government, and it was then that Somerset gained its name as a county, although the origin of that name is not certain. Some sources suggest that the name comes from the Saxon *Seo-mere-saetan* ('dwellers by the sea-lakes'). As we have seen, a good part of Somerset was formerly under the sea, which left huge lakes when the waters receded. Another suggested origin is *Sumortunsaeta,* meaning the people living at, or dependent upon, Sumortun (Somerton). Whichever it is, the first recorded use of the name Somerset occurs in the law code of King Ine of Wessex, which makes it one of the oldest surviving units of local government in the country.

For further convenience, the shires were subdivided into 'Hundreds', each of which consisted of about 100 'hides' (a hide being the amount of land needed to support one family). Somerset had forty of these Hundreds, which included Carhampton, Keynsham, Somerton and Glaston (Glastonbury). 'Hundred courts' would be held monthly to sort out disputes and deal with the less serious crimes. Major crimes could be referred to the 'shire reeve' (sheriff), an officer appointed by the Crown, who was the king's representative and had the responsibility of maintaining the King's Peace within the shire. The earliest Sheriff of Somerset we have a name for is Godwine in 1061; at the time of the Norman invasion it was Tofig, who was still in office two years later.

CROWNING A KING

The first monastic building in Bath was constructed in the seventh century as a convent, and was rebuilt as a monastery by King Offa of Mercia in the eighth. This became the first Bath Abbey on the site, and was such an impressive building that it was chosen for the coronation of King Edgar in 973. At the age of about 30, 'Edgar the Peaceful', as he was known, was crowned 'King of the English', but he would live for only two more years. The ceremony that was devised for that occasion by Dunstan, Archbishop of Canterbury, became the model for all future coronations in England up to the present day.

2

NORMAN SOMERSET: WILLIAM IS NOW IN CHARGE

By the mid-eleventh century the region of Wessex, including Somerset, was under the control of the Saxon Earl Godwin, who, with his two sons, owned a large estate in the county. King Edward the Confessor, seeing them as rebels, banished all three, but in 1052 one of the sons, Harold, returned with an army and landed at Porlock. He defeated the royal forces, and in 1066, following Edward's death, declared himself king. This resulted in the invasion that year by William of Normandy, who believed that the crown had been promised to him. Harold's forces were defeated at Hastings, and William was duly crowned on Christmas Day, 1066. He immediately began rewarding his loyal followers with grants of land that had formerly belonged to Saxon nobles. The Normans also introduced the Feudal System into England, under which the structure of society was a bit like a pyramid, with the king at the top, then the nobility, the knights, and at the bottom, the peasantry. Each level owed obedience and duty to the levels above it. Prominent Norman landowners held *fiefs* (estates) in Somerset, some of which covered a large area. During the Norman period there were about 700 such fiefs in Somerset.

In 1067, King William returned to Normandy and took with him some hostages, among whom was Aethelnoth, the Abbot of Glastonbury, who was kept prisoner until he was finally deposed in 1078 and replaced by a Norman bishop named Thurstan.

In late 1068 the sons of King Harold, who had died at Hastings, sailed from Ireland to the coast of Somerset, where they landed and fought a battle near Bleadon. They were defeated, but succeeded in killing Eadnoth, a Saxon *thegn* who had changed sides and was now fighting for William.

DOMESDAY – IT'S ALL IN THE BOOK!

To further consolidate his position, William commissioned the famous 'Domesday Book', completed in 1086, which contains a detailed survey of most of England (and part of Wales). This was done in order to establish how many people were living in his new kingdom, how much land there was and the amount of tax it had been yielding. The book tells us that in Somerset there were more than 500 'burgesses' (freemen in a borough) and about 12,000 'unfree' people, as well as around 50,000 sheep! The commissioners were charged with recording every manor, who had previously held it, the number of inhabitants – even the farm animals they owned. For example, we learn that Castle Cary, which before the Conquest had been held by a Saxon named Alfsi, comprised enough land for twenty ploughs, had forty-nine inhabitants, sixteen cattle, fifty pigs, 115 sheep, one mill and was worth £15. This information was invaluable to the king, since it told him how much revenue he could expect to get and how many men he might call upon to fight, if necessary. Although most people at this time lived in villages, towns were beginning to grow in number and size. Bath, for instance, probably had a population of about 1,000, while Ilchester, with a population of about 500, would, in the twelfth century, become the county town of Somerset. Its thirteenth-century mace is the oldest staff of office in England.

The Domesday survey for Somerset lists a total of 622 settlements, ranging from *Tantone* (Taunton), which had 479 households and paid £52 4s in tax, to places such as *Bernet* (Burnett, near Keynsham), which had no actual households and paid nothing. Almost half of the settlements recorded in Domesday were of one hide or less. Apart from animals, the only real source of power was water, and Domesday records around 6,000 mills in England, with 371 of them being in Somerset (compared with Cornwall, which had only six).

From the Domesday Survey we can see that the population of Somerset was between 50,000 and 60,000, making it one of only six counties that had more than 50,000 inhabitants. The total population of England at that time stood at around 1¼ million.

RELIGIOUS HOUSES

During the Norman period great abbeys were founded to house the religious orders that were growing in size and importance. The site at **Glastonbury** was, according to medieval legend, founded by Joseph of Arimathea, kinsman of Jesus, who, after the Crucifixion, came with twelve followers to this spot and brought with him the Holy Grail. This was the cup used by Jesus at the Last Supper (although in some versions, Joseph brought two cruets containing the blood and sweat of Christ, see illustration). Earlier, so the legend says, Joseph had brought the young Jesus with him to Somerset, which, centuries later, would inspire the poet William Blake to write:

> And did those feet in ancient time
> Walk upon England's mountains green?
> And was the holy Lamb of God
> On England's pleasant pastures seen?

The abbey itself had its beginnings in the Saxon era, and was rebuilt and extended after the Conquest by the Norman Abbot Thurstan, who kept his Saxon monks in order by employing archers to shoot down anyone who was disobedient! Glastonbury was by then the richest abbey in the land; its income in 1086 was estimated at £874 per year – a colossal sum, equal to many millions today. In 1184 the monastic buildings were destroyed by fire, but they soon began rebuilding, and the abbey would again become one of the largest and wealthiest in England. The community followed the Rule of St Benedict, with its emphasis on poverty, chastity and obedience. In 1191 the monks claimed to have discovered the tomb of King Arthur and his queen, Guinevere, during the rebuilding, and the two skeletons that they unearthed, of a man and a woman, were reburied in front of the high altar. This may have been a clever ploy on the part of the monks, as the subsequent flow of pilgrims brought much-needed revenue to the abbey. Standing among the abbey ruins today, it is easy to feel the centuries dissolving and to experience a strong sense of the past.

Bath Abbey was also a Benedictine foundation, and the first abbey on the site was an Anglo–Saxon foundation (already referred to). After the Conquest it was rebuilt and extended by the Norman Bishop John de Villula to become a large and imposing Norman abbey, housing around forty monks. Traces of the Norman building can still be seen beneath the floor of the present abbey and in one of the arches. The Abbey and its precincts took up a large part of the town, and had ownership of the baths that had been rebuilt on the site of the old Roman complex.

The cathedral we can see today at **Wells** was begun in about 1180 near the site of an old Saxon church that was founded by King Ine of Wessex. In Domesday, Wells

Glastonbury Abbey ruins

is referred to as 'Welle', meaning 'the springs', which rise in the grounds of the Bishop's Palace and give the city its name. In 1136 the newly elected Bishop Robert granted Wells the right to hold fairs and a market (bishops could do that in those days), but records show that these soon became so noisy and disorderly that Robert made his 'displeasure' clear, warning that the Church would punish any who misbehaved.

BATH V WELLS

The first bishopric in Somerset dates back to the early tenth century, and the *cathedra*, or bishop's seat, was located at Wells in the church, which predated the present cathedral. Then, on the death of Bishop Giso in 1088, King William II granted the see to his physician, Bishop John de Villula, on condition that the bishop's seat was transferred to Bath.

This meant that the bishop assumed the role of abbot, with the former abbot becoming the prior. The abbey therefore became a cathedral priory (although it is still known as 'Bath Abbey'). The new bishop began building a great Norman cathedral in Bath on the ruins of the former Saxon abbey church, and so became Bishop of Bath. Later bishops preferred to live in Wells, and great rivalry grew between the two places, particularly over who should elect the bishop. This continued until 1243, when the Pope finally settled the matter rather neatly by ruling that elections for the bishopric should be held in both churches and the title should in future be 'Bishop of Bath *and* Wells' (as it remains to this day).

Many other, smaller, religious houses, occupied by various Orders, existed in Somerset during the Norman period, such as those at Cleeve (the only Cistercian house in Somerset), Muchelney (Benedictine), Barlynch (Augustinian), Charterhouse (Carthusian) and Bridgwater (Franciscan). These were, of course, strictly male orders; for the women there were nunneries at places such as Ilchester, Barrow, Dunster, Cannington and Buckland. All the religious orders tended to follow the similar basic principles as the Benedictines, but sometimes with a different emphasis. For example, the Cistercians (or White Monks) chose to build their religious houses in remote locations, far from the nearest abbey or church. Friars, such as the Franciscans (or Grey Friars), went out into the community to carry out their good works and to spread the Gospel.

Parish churches dating from the Norman period can be found throughout the county in villages such as Brockley, Holcombe, Monksilver and Williton. Of Norman parish churches, three of the best surviving examples in Somerset are at Stogursey, Stoke-sub-Hamdon and Compton Martin. At Culbone, near the Exmoor coast, can be found what is said to be England's smallest church, with a total length of just 35ft (10.7m) and seating for about thirty people. The church is dedicated to Beuno, a Celtic saint, and is mentioned in Domesday.

A MAN OF MANY PARTS

Adelard of Bath, who lived from about 1080 to about 1160, was a scholar and philosopher who introduced many new ideas into England. There's a lot we don't know about him, but from his own writings we learn that he was born in Bath, and other sources suggest he died there. In between, he travelled widely, first to the Continent, where he studied and taught. He then journeyed to Syria and, later, to Palestine. Eventually returning to Bath, he

wrote widely on philosophy, astronomy, botany, zoology and mathematics, and, having learned Arabic, translated a number of texts. He is often credited with introducing the concept of 'zero' into England. He also practised alchemy and astrology. Sometimes regarded as England's first true scientist, one of his books was among the first to be published three centuries later.

STRICTLY FOR THE BIRDS

One of the innovations introduced into England by the Normans was the dovecote. These small buildings were usually circular and had a hole in the roof through which the birds could enter and leave. The keeping of doves or pigeons was a way of ensuring a supply of fresh meat for the family during the winter, but the practice was not popular among the farmers on whose crops the birds would feed. Theft of these birds was considered a serious crime; if you were convicted of a third offence you could be hanged.

A fine example of a Norman dovecote is the one at Blackford, near Minehead, which is said to be the oldest in England. Other examples of medieval dovecotes can be seen at Dunster and Shapwick.

WHO'S WHO IN NORMAN SOMERSET?

If you were one of the 200 or so Norman knights or lords who accompanied Duke William in 1066, and helped in his conquest of England, you could expect to be well rewarded for your trouble. Many Norman nobles who 'came over with the Conqueror' were granted estates in Somerset. Among the most prominent families were:

Gournay. Nigel de Gournay was a follower of King William I and was given manors in north-east Somerset. The family have left their name in some of the local villages, such as Farrington Gurney, Barrow Gurney and Gurney Slade. A later family member, Sir Thomas de Gournay, was involved in the murder of Edward II at Berkeley Castle in 1327, for which his lands were confiscated and given to the Duchy of Cornwall.

Mohun. William de Mohun (or Moyon), accompanied the Conqueror on his invasion, and was granted fifty-five manors in west Somerset, his main seat being at Dunster Castle. He was appointed Sheriff of the county in 1086, and he is credited with founding Dunster Priory. His son, also William, was created the first Earl of Somerset in 1141.

Douai. Walter of Douai probably fought at Hastings and as a result was granted major land holdings in the south-west of England. He became feudal baron of Castle Cary, and was responsible for building the first motte and bailey castle there.

Beauchamp. Robert de Beauchamp and his family were loyal allies of King William, and their name is commemorated in the village of Hatch Beauchamp, near Taunton.

Montfort. The De Montforts were given the manor of Farleigh, near Bath, and held it until the fourteenth century. They named it Farleigh Montfort, but during the reign of Edward III it passed to the Hungerford family and became known as Farleigh Hungerford.

DON'T MESS WITH THE TEMPLARS!

The Order of Poor Knights of the Temple of Solomon, better known as the Knights Templar, also acquired extensive lands in Somerset. These formidable warrior monks, formed during the Crusades to protect the pilgrim routes to the Holy Land, became immensely wealthy and powerful in the twelfth and thirteenth centuries. One of their seals shows two knights riding a single horse, signifying their vow of poverty. They had administrative centres or 'preceptories' throughout the county, and were in the enviable position of being answerable to no one except the Pope. They alone held jurisdiction over their lands, and were extremely able administrators, both in land management and in finance. They were also fearsome warriors, the Special Forces of their day, who vowed not to retreat in battle unless the odds against them exceeded three to one. They originated the system of banking by which a person could deposit a sum of money at a Templar preceptory and withdraw it, or have it paid to a creditor, from another in a different country, thus avoiding the danger and uncertainty of carrying large sums of cash around. In Somerset, the Templar name survives today in locations such as Templecombe and Temple Cloud, and they also had a large holding at Temple Fee (now Temple Meads) in Bristol. In Templecombe, just to the south of the village, are the remains of a Templar preceptory, and in 1945 a painting on wood, showing the head of a bearded man, was discovered in a nearby barn. This painting has been carbon-dated to the thirteenth century, a time when the Templars owned the site, and is thought to represent the head of either Christ or John the Baptist.

Because of their power and influence the Templars gained many enemies, and on Friday, 13 October 1307, Templars throughout France were simultaneously arrested on the orders of the king, Philip IV. Many charges were brought

against them, including the worship of idols, and some confessions were obtained under torture. When the order was finally suppressed throughout Christendom by the Pope in 1312, most of the Templar lands were given to the rival Knights Hospitaller (or Knights of St John), who called their centres of administration 'commanderies'.

KING OF THE CASTLE?

William I also personally oversaw a programme of castle building in order to overawe and subdue his conquered subjects. In Somerset, castles were built at Dunster, Montacute and Neroche, and later at places such as Castle Cary, Stogursey and East Harptree. At first, these castles were simple wooden structures built on a 'motte', or mound of earth, but they were gradually replaced with stone structures. Sometimes they would be built on the sites of former Iron Age hill forts, where they had a commanding position. These castles were occupied by prominent members of the Norman aristocracy (for example, Montacute was owned by Robert of Mortain, who was King William's half-brother). The name 'Montacute' is thought to come from the Latin for 'pointed hill' (*mons acutus*), and may refer to the nearby St Michael's Hill, which is sharply conical.

DUNSTER CASTLE

When, soon after the Conquest, William de Mohun was granted the feudal barony of Dunster he first built a timber 'motte and bailey' castle on the site, but by the early twelfth century this had been replaced by a stone keep that was later remodelled. Early in the Civil War (see below) William's son (also William) successfully defended the castle against a siege by King Stephen's forces, for which a grateful Empress Matilda created him Earl of Somerset. For his actions, William was nicknamed 'the Scourge of the West'.

CIVIL WAR – STEPHEN V MATILDA

Before the death of Henry I in 1135, Stephen (grandson of the Conqueror) had sworn to accept Henry's daughter Matilda as successor to the throne. However, when the time came Stephen grabbed the throne for himself, leading to years of civil war that raged up and down the country, bringing misery and death to many. With no one effectively in control, the barons roamed the country, looting and pillaging at will. It was a period that is sometimes known as 'the Anarchy', when, as one chronicler put it, 'Christ and his saints slept'.

Somerset managed to escape the worst of this trouble, although, in 1138, Stephen, having failed to capture Bristol, brought his forces to attack Richmont Castle at East Harptree, whose owner was a supporter of Matilda. Stephen set up his siege engines a long way from the castle, which encouraged the defenders to come out and attack. Stephen's men then assaulted and burned the castle gates, cutting off any retreat and successfully taking the castle. In 1141, Stephen was himself captured and briefly imprisoned in Bristol Castle.

The conflict lasted for the best part of twenty years, only coming to an end in 1153 when peace was finally negotiated. The deal reached was that Stephen should remain king for the remainder of his lifetime (actually he died the following year), after which Henry (Matilda's son) would succeed to the throne. He did so, as Henry II, in 1154.

THE KING'S HIT SQUAD

In 1168 a Norman knight, Sir Reginald FitzUrse, inherited the manor of Williton. Two years later he was one of the four over-enthusiastic knights who rode to Canterbury and murdered the 'turbulent priest' Archbishop Thomas Becket on the chancel steps of the Cathedral, in the mistaken belief that they were carrying out the wishes of King Henry II. Afterwards, all four were excommunicated and fled the country. FitzUrse sold his manor to the Order of Knights Hospitaller, so as to raise enough money to go on pilgrimage to Rome and the Holy Land to try to atone for his sins. He never returned to England.

SOMERSET AND THE GREAT CHARTER

In July 1215 a group of twenty-five rebel barons forced King John to set his seal to the Great Charter, or 'Magna Carta' as it became known. This important document placed limits on the power of the king, and enshrined in law various liberties for his subjects, such as the right to trial by jury. One of the barons was William Malet, Feudal Baron of Curry Mallet, near Taunton. He had previously fought on crusade alongside Richard I (the Lionheart), but later joined the rebellion against Richard's brother, John. William died a few months after Magna Carta was confirmed. The town of Shepton Mallet is also named after the family. Such was the importance of Magna Carta that it was used in 1776 as the basis for the Declaration of Independence of the United States of America.

3

MEDIEVAL SOMERSET: WOOL AND WEALTH

During the later Middle Ages, great efforts were made in Somerset to increase the amount of land available for food production. Marshes and wetlands were drained and woodlands cleared to create more land to cope with the growing number of mouths needing to be fed. The population of Somerset in 1377 has been estimated at just over 100,000, at a time when that of England as a whole was around 2.5 million. The land reclaimed from the sea was rich and fertile, providing good grazing and productive soil. Farming operated on the mixed farming system – crops and livestock, as today – and also on the open, or 'three-field' system, under which land was shared, with fields divided into strips. One field would be left fallow each year to rest the soil, while the other two were planted with crops, with the use of the fields being rotated every year.

Sheep farming also became increasingly important, and during the thirteenth and fourteenth centuries wool was the mainstay of the English economy (to this day, the Lord Speaker of England sits on a woolsack). The importance of the woollen industry continued well into the seventeenth century, when, to help protect the industry, all bodies had to be buried in shrouds made of English wool. The pasturelands of Somerset provided ideal grazing, and more and more land was given over to the grazing of sheep. Wool merchants became very wealthy, and some towns and villages in Somerset prospered. Dunster is a fine example of such a village. It has a fifteenth-century 'wool church', built and enriched by wealthy locals with profits from the wool trade, and the famous Yarn Market that stands in the High Street was where woollen cloth was bought and sold (although this was built slightly later, in about 1600). Trades associated with the production of woollen cloth, such as spinning, weaving and dyeing, were all local industries giving employment to large numbers of people. Weaving became an important cottage industry, with travelling weavers visiting regularly to weave the

yarn produced by the 'spinsters', (often unmarried) women who spun the wool into cloth in their homes. Sometimes communities of weavers would operate in the same locality, as at Twerton, near Bath (Chaucer's 'Wife of Bath' was a skilled weaver, and may well have lived here). Weavers from Flanders and the Low Countries were also encouraged to come to England to practise their craft, and woollen cloth produced in England was highly prized on the Continent.

Timber was also a vital material, used for building and for the making of such things as hurdles, furniture, tools and, of course, for fuel. Special permission was granted for using timber from royal forests and parks for building and repair work at the castles of Bridgwater and Stogursey, the abbeys of Glastonbury and Cleeve and the prison at Somerton. Wood was also important for use in shipbuilding, with the increasing size of ports such as Watchet and Bridgwater, as well as nearby Bristol. Bridgwater was formally recognised as a port by an act of Parliament passed in 1348. This meant that locally collected taxes could be invested in developing the port, and stone quays, slipways for the launching of ships and a dry dock were constructed. This expansion meant that the local cloth trade could develop, with cloth exports reaching their peak in the early 1500s.

During the Middle Ages some Somerset towns prospered sufficiently to be granted charters, giving them the right to hold regular fairs and markets, to elect members of Parliament and to enjoy certain trading privileges. For a time, during the thirteenth and fourteenth centuries, Somerton became the county town, taking over that role from Ilchester, but its fortunes varied and it was never to grow into a large town.

THE RISE OF TAUNTON

The name of Taunton is a corruption of 'Tone Town' (the town on the River Tone). Even in Saxon times the town was of some importance, being a 'burh' (fortified settlement) in its own right and possessing its own mint. In about AD 700 King Ine of Wessex had built a wooden stronghold here, but that was later burned down by his warrior queen Aethelburg to prevent its falling into the hands of their enemies.

Since before the Conquest, the manor of Taunton had been in the ownership of the Bishop of Winchester, and in AD 904 King Edward the Elder granted it a charter, freeing it from certain taxes.

In the tenth century a priory was built, which in Norman times was converted into the stone structure that became Taunton Castle. At the time of the Domesday Book the population of Taunton was already almost 1,500 (at a time when the average village had about 100 or so inhabitants). The town grew greatly in size between the early thirteenth and early fourteenth centuries. It succeeded Somerton as the county town in the 1360s.

The medieval fairs and markets held in Taunton became famous for the sale of a particular type of woollen cloth known as 'Tauntons', which was produced in the town. Taunton's prosperity can be judged from the fact that by about the beginning of the fifteenth century it was sending two members to Parliament.

Queen Margaret of Anjou passed through the town with her army in 1471 on her way north, in an (unsuccessful) bid to outrun her Yorkist enemies.

A magnificent tower for St Mary Magdalene church was begun in 1488 and financed by local wool merchants. It was restored by Sir George Gilbert Scott in 1862, and on completion, the donkey that had hauled the stone was hoisted to the top, presumably to admire the view!

THE SHERIFF

The office of Sheriff of Somerset has existed for more than 1,000 years, and some well-known names have held the post. From 1083 to 1086 the post was held by our friend William de Mohun of Dunster Castle. Thirteenth-century sheriffs included Hubert de Burgh, Earl of Kent and one of the most powerful men in the country; William Longespée, Earl of Salisbury and half-brother to King John; and Eleanor of Castile, first queen to Edward I. Some sheriffs held the appointment more than once, while in other cases it was subsequently occupied by sons and grandsons.

THE POWER OF THE CHURCH

Religion played a huge part in the lives of medieval men and women, which meant that the Church was one of the most important institutions in the land. In Somerset there were more than 350 parish churches, some having existed since before the Conquest, such as the church of St John the Evangelist at Milborne Port, near the border with Dorset. The village priest was an important member of the community, acting as a shepherd to his flock. Many churches have a list of incumbents dating back almost 1,000 years, with each having left its mark on its small community. The vicar of St Michaels's church at East Coker in 1490 was one John Godefellow (hard to think of a better name for a clergyman)!

Many of the larger churches had specially dedicated chapels and chantries. These latter were built so that regular masses could be 'chanted' for the departed souls of people of note, who would have left endowments to the church stipulating that this should be done to provide them with a kind of 'passport' to heaven.

Abbeys and monasteries, particularly the larger ones such as Bath and Glastonbury, were not only the largest private landowners, but also had a direct effect on the daily lives of the local population. As well as being important religious and spiritual centres, they acted as repositories of knowledge and culture. They also provided education, healthcare and hospitality to travellers – even a place where the homeless or destitute could find help. Many of the abbots, abbesses and bishops were highly enlightened people, who brought about considerable change.

BISHOPS OF BATH AND WELLS

During the middle ages many clergy occupied the prestigious seat of Bath and Wells. Here are some of the most notable holders of the post, together with the dates they were in office:

John De Villula (1088–1123) was also known as John of Tours, and was technically Bishop of Bath only. He was responsible for the building of the great Norman abbey at Bath, the predecessor of the present building.

Reginald Fitz Jocelin (1174–92), like Bishop John, held the seat of Bath. He began the building of Wells Cathedral in about 1180, and started the construction of the Bishop's Palace. In 1191 he was elected Archbishop of Canterbury, but died before he could be installed. He is said always to have worn a hair shirt under his clerical robes as a sign of his piety.

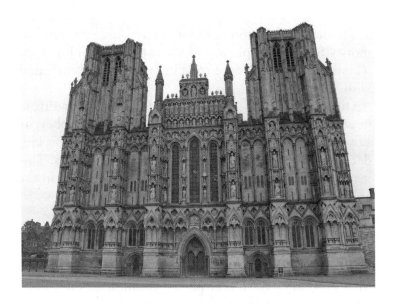

William Bytton II (1267–75) was apparently possessed of remarkably good teeth well into old age, which many attributed to his saintly life. After his death, people suffering from toothache would visit his shrine in the cathedral in the hope of obtaining relief.

Ralph of Shrewsbury (1329–63) was responsible for the building of Vicars' Close near the cathedral, thought to be the oldest complete medieval street in Europe. In his will, on his death in 1363, he left £40 to be distributed among the local poor (probably worth at least £25,000 today). It was during his time as bishop that the famous 'scissor' or strainer arches were erected in the crossing of the nave. The main tower above this was originally much higher and was topped with a wooden spire. By the mid-1300s this huge weight was causing serious damage to the fabric of the building, so these unusually shaped arches were constructed to spread the load from one side to the other.

Thomas Beckington (1443–65) gave large amounts of money for the completion of the cathedral, and had the 'Chain Bridge' across the road built to link the cathedral with Vicars' Close.

Oliver King (1495–1504) claimed to have had a dream in which, standing in the ruins of the Norman Abbey, he saw angels travelling between earth and heaven on ladders, and a voice urging him to restore the church. This inspired him to begin the work in 1499, resulting in the abbey we see today.

ROYAL FOREST

Medieval kings were very partial to hunting, and, since Norman times, had set aside specific areas of land as 'Royal Forests': preserves that were for the exclusive use of the king and his nobles to indulge in their favourite pastime. In Somerset, an area of Exmoor in the west of the county, consisting of about 20,000 acres, was designated a Royal Forest, possibly during the reign of Henry II (1154–89). Forest laws against hunting by commoners were savage; those caught could expect to lose an eye or a hand. Even dogs that were taken into the forest had to be 'lawed', that is, to have some of the claws and pads on their forefeet removed so that they could not chase after the deer. These laws were enforced by the Forest Wardens, who were paid by the Crown.

THE TARR STEPS MYSTERY

Spanning the River Barle near Withypool is Tarr Steps, a bridge of the type known as a 'clapper', that is, made from large flat stones balanced on others sitting on the riverbed. But when was it built? Opinions differ on this, with some suggesting that it dates from the Bronze Age. Most experts today, however, believe that it was constructed in the late medieval period, as the first written reference to it dates from the fourteenth century. It is the longest bridge of its kind in Britain. Local tradition insists that it was built by the Devil, who was in the habit of sunbathing on it!

BLACK DEATH

This terrible plague reached England in June 1348, coming in through the nearby county of Dorset and quickly reaching Somerset. It took a heavy toll on the population, virtually wiping out whole villages. In Crowcombe, for example, rental payments fell by 97 per cent, while the population of Shepton Mallet was reduced to fewer than 300. Some estimates suggest that, in all, as much as 46 per cent of the population of England died in the space of three years. The number of people succumbing (and this included clergy) was so great that there were not enough priests to hear so many victims' confessions, and large numbers were dying unshriven. To get around this problem Ralph of Shrewsbury, Bishop of Bath and Wells, took the unprecedented step of allowing lay people to hear each other's confessions, even extending this privilege to women – but only if no man was present! He also ordered that every parish church should organise a weekly service during which people should 'abase themselves humbly' and pray that God would 'turn away from His people this pestilence'. Bishop Ralph himself retired to his house in Wiveliscombe while the plague was raging. Who can blame him? An unprecedented number of clergy were struck down. Church records show that in the years 1348–49 two rectors were installed at Uphill and two at Weston-super-Mare, while as many as four vicars were appointed at Worle. The vicar of Kewstoke died in 1348. The plague did not discriminate between the social classes.

To add to people's woes, during this period there was also a succession of poor harvests due to bad weather. The upside of all this was that, with the scarcity of labour once things had returned to normal, workers could demand higher wages and better conditions. This in turn resulted in increased food prices. Some estates were broken up, and a general movement away from the old Feudal System to a much freer arrangement got under way. Many peasants were released from serfdom and were now free to move to where they could achieve a better standard of living, and so the rural population gradually became less static. The plague continued to return at intervals throughout the medieval period and afterwards.

THE PEASANTS ARE REVOLTING!

In May 1381 the men of Essex and Kent rose up against the injustice of the tax system and, together with their leader, Wat Tyler, marched on London. Thus began a period of social unrest that became known as the Peasants' Revolt.

Several important officials were murdered, including Simon of Sudbury, Archbishop of Canterbury. The rebels finally met with the 14-year-old King Richard II and his retinue at Smithfield, where Tyler was killed. This, however, was not the end of the 'summer of blood', as it has been called. The rebellion spread to other areas of the country, and by 19 June had reached Somerset. After a public demonstration in Bridgwater marketplace there were two days of violent disorder in the town. A mob led by Thomas Engilby and Adam Brugge then marched to St John's Hospital, which they threatened to burn down unless they were given the money and tithes due to the church. After receiving these, they attacked and burned properties belonging to John Sydenham, a wealthy merchant, and Thomas Duffeld, Bridgwater's leading lawyer. They subsequently murdered local men Walter Baron and Hugh Lavenham, and mounted their heads on spikes on the town bridge. They finally moved on to Ilchester, where they stormed the town gaol and released many of the prisoners. When news was received that the rebellion in other parts of the country had been crushed, Engilby fled the country. In his absence he was condemned to death (but was later pardoned).

After this, things seem to have quietened down, but the outrage left a black mark on Bridgwater, which was one of the last towns in England to be pardoned when a general amnesty was issued later in the year.

AN ENGLISHMAN'S HOME IS ...

The programme of castle building begun by the Normans was continued during the fourteenth and fifteenth centuries, as the prospect of invasion or civil insurrection was never very far away. Although Somerset was some distance away from the centre of political events, some local magnates felt the need to provide themselves with strong defences against possible attack. The most effective way was to build a castle or obtain a licence to 'crenellate' or fortify an existing manor house.

Dunster Castle

This castle, as we have seen, was begun by the de Mohuns in the twelfth century and was gradually enlarged and extended. In the fourteenth century it was inherited by Sir John de Mohun. He and his wife were childless, and Sir John ran up large debts. On his death in 1376 his widow, Joan, sold the castle to Lady Elizabeth Luttrell for 3,000 marks (roughly £850,000 today). The Luttrells, another important Norman family, then occupied it until the twentieth century. It is now managed by the National Trust.

Nunney Castle

This moated castle near Frome dates from the 1370s, and is one of the smallest in Britain. It was built for Sir John

Delamare, a noted soldier in the Hundred Years' War, during which he had gained a fortune from the ransoming of captives. A one-time High Sheriff of Somerset, he sought and received permission from Edward III to build a castle on the site of his existing manor house. A medieval castle in miniature, complete with a moat, Nunney is now a picturesque ruin and is a scheduled monument in the care of Historic England. It played a part in the English Civil War, as we shall see later.

Farleigh Hungerford Castle

Built in the late fourteenth century for Sir Thomas Hungerford, steward to John of Gaunt, it was (like Nunney) raised on the site of a former manor house. A neighbouring village was destroyed in order to create a park. Sir Thomas's son, Sir Walter, was a courtier of Henry V, and fought alongside him at the battle of Agincourt in 1415. He extended the castle, which remained in the family's hands for another two centuries, until gambling debts forced them to sell it.

Clevedon Court

The building of this small manor house was begun in the early fourteenth century by Sir John de Clevedon. Sir John may have been a descendant of Matthew de Mortagne, who had been granted the manor of Clevedon by William the Conqueror. When the de Clevedon line ended in 1376 the manor passed to the Wakes, a Northamptonshire family, who held it for nearly 300 years. In 1709 the property was bought by a Bristol merchant, Abraham Elton. The Elton family still live in the house, although it was given to the National Trust in part payment of death duties in 1961.

Ashton Court

It is thought that a fortified manor house existed on this site during the eleventh century, having been given to Geoffrey de Mowbray, Bishop of Coutances, by the Conqueror. It is described in the Domesday Book as a 'wealthy estate', and in the fourteenth century was greatly expanded by the addition of a deer park. After passing through a succession of owners, in 1545 it came into the possession of the Smyth family, who held it for 400 years. It was eventually sold in 1959 to Bristol City Council, which still owns it.

Lytes Cary Manor

This delightful manor house dates from the fourteenth century, and was built by the Lyte family and occupied by them for more than 400 years. Henry Lyte (*c*.1529–1607) was a renowned botanist and antiquary. In 1578 he produced a history of plants entitled *A Niewe Herball,* which

he dedicated to Elizabeth I. The manor's chapel, with its 'squint' window, predates the house itself. The site of a deserted medieval settlement lies within the parkland that surrounds the house. The property is now in the care of the National Trust.

LIFE ON THE LAND

One of the biggest changes to take place in Somerset during the Middle Ages was the increase in the amount of usable farmland, brought about by extensive drainage schemes, especially on the Levels. This brought many hundreds of extra acres into use for the growing of crops and the grazing of sheep and cattle. The first attempts at draining and reclaiming land was probably carried out in the seventh century when the foundations of the original Muchelney Abbey were being laid. Much of the later work of reclamation was also carried out by monks on behalf of the Church, which was the biggest private landowner in the county. A good example of this is the River Brue, which was diverted into a new channel by the monks of Glastonbury in the Middle Ages in order to drain the low-lying area which was prone to flooding, and would sometimes endanger the Abbey itself.

LANCASTER V YORK: THE WARS OF THE ROSES

For much of the fifteenth century, two powerful factions were competing for the right to wear the English Crown. The origins of the dispute go back a long way, but the problem really centred on the fact that both sides could claim direct descent from King Edward III. The whole thing came to a head when Richard, Duke of York, asserted his right to the throne and rebelled against the King, the weak and ineffectual Henry VI. The nobles then chose sides, some supporting York and declaring their allegiance by wearing the badge of a white rose, while others stood with the Lancastrian King Henry, taking the red rose as their emblem. The action really started in 1455 with the first Battle of St Albans, and continued on and off for the next thirty years, with each side occasionally gaining the upper hand. Eventually the Yorkists met defeat on the field of Bosworth in 1485.

Taunton was the scene of a confrontation between the two rival factions in the shapes of Baron Bonville and Thomas de Courtenay, 13th Earl of Devon. Courtenay had been married (while still a boy) to Lady Margaret Beaufort, mother of the future Henry VII, but supported the Yorkist cause. His near neighbour in Somerset was William, 1st Baron Bonville, a Lancastrian with whom he had been carrying on a long-term feud. In 1451, Courtenay besieged Bonville (who had taken refuge in Taunton Castle) with a force of about 5,000 men. However, when Richard, Duke of York, arrived on the scene, he managed to defuse the situation before any real damage could be done.

In 1471, Margaret of Anjou, Henry VI's queen, made her way through Somerset with her army, on her way to Bristol, where she was refused entry. She therefore continued northward, intending to cross the River Severn and join forces with Jasper Tudor, King Henry's half-brother. However, she met King Edward IV's forces at Tewkesbury, where she suffered final defeat.

ROYAL VISITS – TWO HENRYS COME TO BATH

King Henry VI reigned from 1422 to 1461, and after being deposed by Edward IV, was briefly restored to the throne from 1470 to 1471. During the earlier part of his reign he came to Bath (although the exact date of this visit is not known). Visiting the Baths, the pious and prudish king was shocked by the sight of naked men in the water. John Blacman, Henry's personal confessor, wrote that the King was 'displeased, and went away quickly, abhorring such nudity as a great Offence'.

Edward IV's daughter, Elizabeth of York, married Henry Tudor, Earl of Richmond, who took the throne as Henry VII in 1485. The king visited Bath on three occasions. In 1496 he called in at the city on his way to Bristol, where he would give his blessing to the Italian explorer John Cabot, who would set sail the following year. In 1497 Henry made a formal visit to Bath, which was recorded as an occasion of great pomp and splendour.

A TRAGIC FAMILY

In 1475 Margaret Plantagenet was born at Farleigh Hungerford castle. She was the only surviving daughter of George, Duke of Clarence, who, three years later, was executed for treason on the orders of his brother Edward IV. In 1499 her brother, the Earl of Warwick, went to the block in the Tower because, as the last legitimate Plantagenet heir, he was thought by many to have a better right to the throne than the reigning king, Henry VII. Margaret had an impressive pedigree; she was also heir to the earls of both Warwick and Salisbury. Nonetheless, she was later seen as a possible threat to Henry VIII's position, and so was convicted of treason on the flimsiest of evidence. After spending two and a half years in the Tower, she was subjected to a shamefully bungled execution on Tower Green in 1541 at the age of 62.

4

TUDOR SOMERSET: A RELIGIOUS MELTING POT

Following the defeat of Richard III at Bosworth in 1485, the country entered into the exciting but unsettled Tudor period. Many of the old aristocrats had perished during the Wars of the Roses, and a new aristocracy, drawn from the ranks of the middle classes, was arising. It was a period of expansion and discovery in which Somerset played its part. Bridgwater grew as a port; its merchants traded with Ireland, France, Spain and Portugal, bringing in cargoes of wine, coal, iron, fish and fruit. The trade guilds grew, and towns such as Wells, Taunton, Frome and Yeovil had small communities of foreign workers from France and the Low Countries, often engaged in trades connected with wool, such as weaving, fulling and dyeing.

THE WOULD-BE KING

During Henry VII's reign (1485–1509), various rival claimants to the throne appeared, the most notable being Lambert Simnel and Perkin Warbeck. Neither attempt was successful. Warbeck (who claimed to be Richard, Duke of York, the younger of the two 'Princes in the Tower', and therefore the rightful heir) landed in the West Country in September, 1497. Here he quickly gathered an enthusiastic army of Cornishmen who proclaimed him king. With them, he marched towards London, but, on hearing that King Henry had sent a large force to oppose him, he lost his nerve and deserted his 'army'. He was later captured at Beaulieu in Hampshire, and was brought to Taunton in October 1497, where the King was waiting to receive his surrender. Henry had spent one night in Wells, where he was so annoyed at the sympathy shown there for Warbeck that he fined the town £314. Warbeck was sent to the Tower of London, where, after an unsuccessful escape attempt, he was hanged. There is a pub in Taunton named the Perkin Warbeck.

MONASTERIES: NOW YOU SEE THEM ...

Henry VIII's desperate desire for a male heir led him to seek a divorce from his queen, Katherine of Aragon, who had not produced the required son. His failure to achieve the Pope's agreement to the divorce brought about Henry's decision to break with the Church of Rome, and to declare himself head of the Church in England. A period of reformation began, in which all monasteries and similar religious houses in the country were closed, beginning in 1536 with the dissolution of the smaller ones and, three years later, moving on to the larger ones. 'Hit squads' organised by Thomas Cromwell were sent out to carry out the work of eviction. Cromwell, nicknamed 'the Hammer of the Monks', was Henry's chief minister and, in effect, his deputy. Monks were pensioned off and all the wealth of the abbeys became the property of the Crown. This resulted in an enormous revenue in land and riches for the King (Glastonbury Abbey, for example, had an annual income of around £4,000, about £1.2 million today). Among the smaller religious houses to be closed in Somerset were Muchelney, Hinton and Athelney, while the larger ones included Bath, Glastonbury and Keynsham. One of the unfortunate results of these closures was the disappearance of the welfare and charity work that had been carried out by the monks and their lay brethren.

A GRISLY DEATH

The last English abbey to be closed was that of Glastonbury, said to be the wealthiest in England. In November 1539 Richard Whiting, the 78-year-old abbot, was tried at Wells on a trumped-up charge of treason, using 'evidence' supposedly discovered by Thomas Cromwell's men. The verdict was a foregone conclusion; he was found guilty and dragged on a hurdle through the streets of Glastonbury. Then, together with two of his monks, Roger James and John Thorn, he was taken to the top of Glastonbury Tor, where all three suffered the terrible fate of hanging, drawing and quartering. The four parts of Whiting's body were then sent to Wells, Bath, Bridgwater and Ilchester for public display, and his head was set over the gateway of the abbey. The abbey itself was stripped and plundered and its library trashed. The picturesque abbey ruins today are a poignant reminder of those turbulent and dangerous times.

'HE PUT IN HIS THUMB ...'

The village of Mells played a curious part in the Dissolution. According to a local story, Abbot Whiting gave his steward, a certain Thomas Horner, the task of carrying the deeds of several Somerset manors to London (some versions say they were concealed in a large pie) as a gift for the King. On the way, Horner opened the pie and took out the deeds of Mells Manor, keeping them for himself. Records show that the manor came into the possession of the Horner family around that time, although they may simply have bought the deeds from the abbey. Whatever the truth, the story was immortalised in the nursery rhyme *Little Jack Horner*.

FROM SOMERSET TO FAME

From 1518 to 1523, the Bishop of Bath and Wells was the famous Cardinal Thomas Wolsey (1473–1530). Born the son of an Ipswich butcher, his rise to power had been swift. Ordained in 1498, by 1514 he was already Archbishop of York, and had been appointed Almoner to King Henry VIII. In the same year the Pope created him a cardinal.

During the early years of Henry's reign, Wolsey became a significant figure in almost all matters of state. In 1515 he was appointed by Henry to the post of Lord Chancellor of England. However, his inability to negotiate Henry's divorce from Catherine of Aragon caused him to fall from grace with the King, and led to his subsequent downfall. He was dispossessed of his palace at Hampton Court, and died in disgrace in Leicester at the age of 57.

From 1531 to 1533 the Archdeacon of Taunton was Thomas Cranmer (1489–1556), a man then in his early forties. During his time there he lived in The Old House, Milverton. In 1533 he became the first Protestant Archbishop of Canterbury, having been supportive of Henry VIII in his desire to have his marriage to Catherine of Aragon annulled. The family of Henry's second wife, Anne Boleyn, are believed to have been influential in securing Cranmer's appointment.

Things did not end well for him, however. During the reign of Henry's daughter Mary, Catholicism once again became the state religion, and Cranmer, together with some fellow clerics, was accused and convicted of heresy, and suffered the extreme penalty. He was burned at the stake at Oxford in March 1556 at the age of 66.

A TUDOR HARRY POTTER?

Throughout the centuries, mystics and alchemists have been obsessed with the idea of discovering the Philosopher's Stone: the elusive substance that can allegedly turn base metals into gold. Such a man was Thomas Charnock, who lived during the reigns of Henry VIII and his daughter Elizabeth I. Although Kentish by birth, he spent most of his life in Combwich, near Bridgwater. He had many interests, including astrology and navigation, but was mainly concerned with alchemy, and was convinced he could discover the secret of making gold if only he could escape life's distractions. He wrote to the Queen, asking to be allowed to carry out his researches in peace in the Tower of London, but the request was turned down.

Charnock was very unpopular with his Somerset neighbours, who regarded him with superstitious hostility, not helped by his boasting that he was a master of the dark arts. He died in 1581 and is buried in Otterhampton church. After his death it was said that, for many years, no one was prepared to live in his former cottage.

THE LIE OF THE LAND

Between 1538 and 1543, the poet, antiquary and royal librarian John Leland travelled through much of Somerset while compiling his *Itineraries*, a series of journeys through parts of England in which he recorded anything of interest he found. He was the first person to suggest that the hill fort at South Cadbury was a possible location for King Arthur's Camelot. His notes were not published until long after his death, but they give an interesting picture of the county as it appeared in his time, and he has been called 'the father of English local history'. He described much of Somerset as being 'very fair and fruitful', but noted how much of the previously open country was being enclosed by hedgerows, and how many of the 'open fields' were disappearing, mostly for pasture. As he put it: 'most part of all Somersetshire is in hedgerows enclosed'. He also commented on the number of splendid manor houses that were being built or extended by families who were anxious to show off their increasing wealth and social position.

A TUDOR ENGLISHMAN'S 'DES RES'

During the Tudor period, Somerset's grandest houses were occupied by influential and aristocratic families, and today many of them still reflect the wealth and importance of their former owners. They include:

Barrington Court

Located near Ilminster, this imposing house was begun around 1538 and was originally the home of the Daubeney family who were prominent figures at the English court. Henry Daubeney, Earl of Bridgwater, became bankrupt and the house was sold. It then passed through a succession of owners before being acquired by the National Trust in 1907.

Montacute House

This house was built in about 1598 for Sir Edward Phelips, a wealthy lawyer who went on to become Speaker of the House of Commons. The land had been bought by his great-grandfather, Thomas, from the Cluniac monks of the nearby Montacute Priory. Sir Edward went on to play a key role as prosecutor in the trials of Sir Walter Raleigh in 1603 and of Guy Fawkes and the gunpowder plotters three years later. Like many Elizabethan mansions, Montacute is built on the plan of an 'E' shape. It is also now a National Trust property.

Combe Sydenham Hall

This is an Elizabethan manor house near Stogumber, built around 1580 for Sir George Sydenham, Sheriff of Somerset. His daughter, Elizabeth, became the first wife of the great seaman Sir Francis Drake. The house probably stands on the site of medieval monastic buildings that were connected with Cleeve Abbey.

Brympton D'evercy

The original house was begun in 1220, although little from that period remains today. Originally owned by the d'Evercys, a Norman family, the house was enlarged in the fifteenth and sixteenth centuries by the Sydenham family, one of England's largest landowners. The north wing (known as the Henry VIII wing) was built in about 1520.

Hinton House

This stands near the village of Hinton St George, near Crewkerne, and was originally built as a 'hall house' during the medieval period. In about 1500 it was rebuilt by Sir Amyas Paulet (or Poulett), and was described by a contemporary as 'a right goodly manor place'. Sir Amyas, who died in 1538, had rebelled against Richard III and fought for Henry Tudor (later Henry VII) at Bosworth. He was knighted after the Battle of Stoke (1487). When Catherine of Aragon came to England in 1501 he was one of the gentlemen who provided her escort. There is a story that he had the young Thomas (later Cardinal) Wolsey put into the stocks for taking part in a drunken brawl; certainly there was no love lost between the two men.

His grandson, another Sir Amyas, was a protegé of Sir Francis Walsingham and became a member of the Privy Council under Elizabeth I. He was appointed guardian (in effect, jailer) to Mary, Queen of Scots, when she was confined to Chartley Manor in Staffordshire, before being moved to Fotheringhay Castle, Northamptonshire, where she was beheaded on 8 February 1587.

King John's Hunting Lodge

This timber-framed, late medieval (about 1470) wool merchant's house stands in the town of Axbridge, and actually has no connection with King John. It was never (as far as we know) used for hunting, and is not strictly speaking a lodge! It was formerly occupied by a variety of shops, and now houses a museum of local history. The origin of its name is not known, but it might refer to the fact that there was once a carved 'king's head' on the side of the building, part of which once housed a pub of that name.

Nailsea Court

This house may date from the late fifteenth century, and by 1574 was the home of George Percivale. His son Richard (*c*.1550–1620) became a fluent Spanish speaker, and was able to decipher secret Spanish documents for Sir Francis Walsingham, Elizabeth I's spymaster, giving advance warning of the proposed Spanish Armada.

DUKES OF SOMERSET

The earldom of Somerset was created by the Empress Matilda in 1141, and granted to William de Mohun, whom we have already met. It afterwards passed to the Beaufort family, and became a dukedom in 1443 under Henry VI.

The first Duke of Somerset was John Beaufort (1404–44). The Beauforts were the children of John of Gaunt's marriage to his mistress, Katherine Swynford, who became his third wife in 1396. Because these children had been born before the marriage they had been illegitimate, but were legitimised when the couple were married. However, a condition of this was that they could never succeed to the throne. The dukedom eventually passed to Henry Fitzroy, an illegitimate son of Henry VIII, but he died without issue, and the title was later bestowed on the Seymour family.

When Henry VIII died in 1547 his only legitimate son, Edward, succeeded him as Edward VI. At the time he was only 9 years old, so could not rule independently. Henry had appointed a council to assist him, and the young king's uncle, Edward Seymour, Duke of Somerset, was appointed Lord Protector of England (in effect, ruler), until Edward should reach the age of 18. Seymour was the brother of Jane Seymour, Henry's third wife. However, his personal ambition, coupled with the huge cost of his unsuccessful attempts to conquer Scotland, put him out of favour with the council and made him generally unpopular. He was arrested on various charges and confined for a while in the Tower of London, before finally being beheaded on Tower Hill in January 1552.

The dukedom has remained in the Seymour family up to the present time.

SOMERSET'S CHAMPION WALKER

Thomas Coryate (or Coryat) was born at Crewkerne in about 1577, and brought up in the village of Odcombe, where his father was rector. After attending Winchester College, and then Oxford, he went up to Court, where he became a kind of jester/companion to the 8-year-old Prince Henry (eldest son of the newly crowned James I).

After five years at Court he decided to travel, and undertook a journey through Europe, getting lifts on the outward trip but walking back from Venice to Flushing, a distance of around 1,000 miles. On his return to Somerset he hung up the shoes he had worn (or what was left of them!) in Odcombe church, where a replica pair can still be seen, together with his memorial. He published an account of his travels in a book called *Coryat's Crudities*, published in 1611. Coryate is also credited with reintroducing the fork into English dining, having seen its use in Italy.

In 1612 he set off on his travels again, this time through Asia, but died of dysentery in the town of Surat, India, in 1617.

THE 'INVINCIBLE' ARMADA

In 1588 the bitter animosity between Protestant England and Catholic Spain came to a head when Philip II sent a fleet of 130 ships with the intention of supporting the Spanish army in an invasion of England. The aim was to depose Elizabeth I and make England a Catholic country once again. Thanks to Sir Francis Walsingham, head of Queen Elizabeth's elaborate spy network, these plans were already known, and preparations were made to deal with the proposed attack. Walsingham had two 'intelligencers' at the Spanish court who regularly reported back to him on Spain's intentions.

These preparations had been in progress for some time. The Navy was strengthened, with 300 men from Somerset being levied for the purpose. The principal landed gentry of Somerset had formed an association with the aim of raising troops for the national defence. Even the Church helped. The churchwardens' accounts for Banwell in 1560 record entries for the purchase of 'Bowes, a Sheyffe of Arrowes and a Sworde' (total cost 13*s* and 4*d*). In 1586 the rector of Weston-super-Mare contributed £3 2*s* 6*d* towards expenses for the preparations.

Surveys were carried out in various counties to assess the number of potential troops available. In Somerset, 12,000 men were judged as 'able-bodied', with about 4,000 assessed as trained and armed (about half with firearms). Somerset was home to quite a number of old soldiers who

had served in Spain, Ireland and the Low Countries, and these were very experienced. One of these men was Roger Sydenham, who had seen service in Flanders and had also fought in Ireland under the Earl of Essex. When the sailing of the Armada was reported, they all, together with fifty lancers and 100 light horsemen, marched to London to defend the city.

Preparations were made for moving large bodies of men, should the Spanish try to land, depending on where the landing took place. If Plymouth or Falmouth proved to be the landing place, Somerset was to send 3,000 men to support those of Devon and Cornwall. If it should be Poole, then 4,000 Somerset men would be sent as reinforcements.

Bridgwater provided a ship called the *William,* which, with a crew of forty, was sent to join Sir Francis Drake at Plymouth. Chard contributed towards fitting out and manning the *Revenge* (Drake's own ship) and the *Jacobe.* On 21 July, news of the sighting of the Armada was brought to Bridgwater by a ship that had spotted the fleet three days earlier. Beacon fires were lit throughout the country to spread the word. In Somerset, these were located on high points such as Dunkery, Selworthy, and Crook Peak on Mendip.

With the defeat of the Armada in August 1588, celebrations were held in many Somerset towns, including Taunton.

A PATRIOTIC PIRATE

Sir Amyas Preston (d. 1617) was born in Cricket St Thomas to a well-established family. He went to sea as a young man and was a lieutenant in the *Ark* that fought against the Armada, an action in which he was seriously wounded. He then became a privateer (a kind of legalised pirate with authority to attack any enemy ships), and voyaged to the Spanish Main, plundering Spanish possessions as he went. He sacked the town of Santiago de Leon (now Caracas), then returned to England, where he was knighted in 1597. From then until his death he held the post of Keeper of the Ordnance at the Tower of London. In his novel *Westward Ho!* (1855), Charles Kingsley based the character of his hero, Amyas Leigh, on Preston.

'UNWILLINGLY TO SCHOOL'

Most education at this time was under the control of the Church and the monasteries, where pupils were taught the rudiments of reading, writing and calculating. The earliest such school in Somerset is Wells Cathedral School, founded in 909 and one of the oldest in Europe. The first independent schools in Somerset began to appear in the thirteenth century. A school with about twenty pupils is recorded at St John's Hospital, Bridgwater, in 1298, and in 1379 the town had a 'Master of Schools'.

Grammar schools such as that of Taunton, founded by Bishop Foxe in 1522, provided a Latin-based education, but after the Dissolution and the disappearance of the monasteries, grammar schools that were independent of the church began to appear. Henry VIII had allowed some of the money from the former monasteries to be used to replace grammar schools that had been lost, such as the one that had been run by Bath Abbey, and in 1552 King Edward's School was established in Bath.

5

STUART SOMERSET: KING V PARLIAMENT

WATER, WATER EVERYWHERE ...

In January 1607 a huge tidal surge sent the waters of the Bristol Channel far inland and caused extensive flooding. Sea walls were breached, and the floods spread as far inland as Glastonbury, causing the landscape to look much as it must have done centuries earlier. It's thought that as many as 3,000 people may have died as a result. In the church at Kingston Seymour, which lies below sea level, a plaque records the event, and states that: 'many Persons were drowned and much Cattle and Goods were lost; the Water in the Church was five feet high, and the greatest part lay on the Ground about ten days'.

DRAINING THE LEVELS

Something needed to be done to alleviate the persistent problems caused by flooding in the area known as the Levels. Enter Cornelis Vermuyden (1595–1677), a Dutch engineer with considerable experience in the Netherlands of reclaiming large areas of land from the sea. He came to England in about 1620 and became an English citizen. Initially he worked in East Anglia draining the Fens, and in 1629 he received a knighthood. During the reign of James I much of Sedgemoor had come into Crown ownership, and in 1632 Charles I sold 4,000 acres of the Somerset moorland to Vermuyden and Jeffrey Kirby, a London businessman. Then, after the Civil War, in about 1655, the Dutchman sought Oliver Cromwell's permission to drain his portion of the 'boggy and unwholesome' area of Sedgemoor. However, when the Bill came before Parliament it was rejected because of local opposition from some freeholders and tenants (the 'nimbys' of their day), and Vermuyden sold his share of the moor. If he had been allowed to go ahead with his plans, the elaborate and expensive drainage schemes undertaken in the following century (which included digging the great King's Sedgemoor Drain) would probably have been unnecessary.

'CIVILE WARRES' (1642–51)

The growing division between King and Parliament finally came to a head in 1642. King Charles I's belief in the 'divine right of kings' did not sit well with the English Parliament. After Charles had tried (unsuccessfully) to arrest five members of the House of Commons for treason, people began choosing sides, and fighting soon broke out. At first many areas remained neutral, but gradually more and more sections of society declared for either the King or Parliament. Broadly speaking, the cities and larger centres of population supported Parliament, while the rural and less developed areas were for the King. However, many chose not to join the conflict; it has been estimated that only about 20 to 25 percent of adult males in the country actually took an active part.

Somerset was divided in its allegiance, with the north largely supporting Parliament and the south rallying to the royalist cause. Taunton and Bridgwater, for example, were for Parliament, while Wells supported the King. Friends and families, too, were torn apart. A sad example of this happened during the storming of Wardour Castle, just on the border with Wiltshire, where in 1644 a young royalist musketeer named Hilsdean was mortally wounded by his own brother, who was fighting on the opposing side.

Encouraged by successes in Cornwall and Devon, the Royalist forces under Sir Ralph Hopton gathered strength and forced the towns of Taunton, Bridgwater and Dunster to surrender. They then moved on towards Bath, where the opposing armies met at Lansdown.

The Battle of Lansdown (5 July 1643)

This was fought on Lansdown Hill, just outside Bath, between the forces of Sir Ralph Hopton (Royalist) and Sir William Waller (Parliamentarian). Hopton and Waller had been close friends, and now found themselves on opposing sides. A poignant letter survives, written by Waller to his friend Hopton before the battle, in which he deplores the fact that they must oppose each other, and hates 'this warr without an Enemie', but assuring him that there is no personal animosity between them ('Wee are both upon the Stage, and must act those Parts that are assigned to us in this Tragedy.')

Waller had chosen a good position at the top of the hill, and Hopton's forces attacked, but sustained heavy losses. Despite fierce fighting, during which one of the Royalist commanders, the Cornishman Sir Bevil Grenville, was killed, they could not dislodge Waller's troops, who were sheltered behind a wall. That night, under cover of darkness, Waller retreated to Bath, leaving lighted matches stuck into the wall to give the impression that his forces were still there. The ruse worked; when one of Hopton's men was offered a reward for crawling forward to reconnoitre, he found no sign of the enemy.

After the Civil War, Hopton was exiled to Bruges in Belgium, where he died in 1652. Waller became a politician, and died at his estate in Middlesex in 1668.

The Battle of Langport (10 July 1645)

This was the battle in which Parliament gained control over the west of England, defeating the last Royalist field army and heralding the end of the First Civil War. The Royalists, numbering about 7,000 and under the command of General George Goring, made a stand near the small town of Langport, hoping to halt the advance of Cromwell's New Model Army, around 10,000 in number and led by Sir Thomas Fairfax. However, the Royalists were not only heavily outnumbered but also outgunned, and in a few hours the battle was over. After suffering heavy casualties the King's forces retreated, with Goring setting fire to Langport in an attempt to hinder pursuit. Many of the fugitives were captured, and some were killed by angry locals.

The Siege of Nunney (September 1645)

In August 1645 a large force of Parliamentarians, under the command of Sir Thomas Fairfax, laid siege to the Royalist-held Nunney Castle. The siege lasted for several days, during which, according to some versions, the defenders brought a young pig to one of the towers each day, where they pulled its ears and tail, causing it to squeal loudly. This, they hoped, would trick their attackers into thinking they were slaughtering a pig every day, and thus had plentiful supplies of food. However, Fairfax's men were not fooled, and Nunney Castle surrendered when heavy ordnance was brought up and a huge breach made in one of its walls. The damage can still be seen today.

The fortunes of the two sides ebbed and flowed in Somerset, and in late 1644 the Parliamentary army tried to recapture the West Country. Several of Somerset's main towns were besieged and eventually forced to surrender, with their leaders taken prisoner. Dunster was the last to capitulate, after having held out for 160 days, but in the end the castle's governor, Francis Wyndham, was forced to give in. Regrettably, during all the activity of the Civil War years, the behaviour in Somerset of troops on both sides seems to have left a lot to be desired, with some contemporary writers complaining bitterly about ill treatment.

TAUNTON

Taunton, as we have seen, grew from a Saxon burh to become Somerset's county town by the fourteenth century. In 1627 the town was granted a new charter by Charles I, freeing it from the control of the Bishop of Winchester and allowing it to elect a mayor and civic corporation. This charter was revoked by Charles II when he came to the throne in 1660, because the town had opposed his father and supported Parliament during the Civil War, but he reinstated it in 1677. He also ordered that Taunton Castle should be 'slighted' (that is, partially destroyed) so that it could not be used against him in the future.

SOMERSET SEADOGS

By the Tudor period Bristol had established itself as a major trading port, and many voyages of exploration set off from here. However, seamen from ports such as Bridgwater, Minehead and Watchet were well acquainted with the dangers of the Atlantic. In 1543 Minehead had at least eight large vessels, with a total crew of seventy-seven men. As well as trading regularly with France, Spain and Portugal, some Somerset sailors ventured farther afield, making the voyage to Newfoundland and the Grand Banks in search of cod. Somerset families were also instrumental in colonising the New World; Sir Ferdinando Gorges from Wraxall was granted land in what is now Maine in 1628 and, though he never set foot in America himself, he was responsible for setting up a colony there. The area of land he colonised was originally given the name of New Somersetshire, and today there is still a Somerset County in the state of Maine.

WHIPPING THE ENEMY

Robert Blake was born near Bridgwater in 1598. He attended Wadham College, Oxford (where his portrait hangs), and after a period in trade, stood for and was elected Member of Parliament for Bridgwater. During the Civil War he joined Cromwell's New Model Army, rising to the rank of colonel and distinguishing himself in several actions, including the sieges of Bristol, Taunton and Dunster. While defending Taunton against the Royalists he vowed he'd eat two of his three pairs of boots before he'd surrender. Fortunately for his digestion, he managed to hold out!

In 1649 he was appointed 'General at Sea' (in effect, Admiral), and is sometimes called the 'Father of the Royal Navy'. During the Anglo–Dutch War of 1652–53, the Dutch Admiral, Maarten Tromp, following a victory off Dungeness, allegedly tied a broom to his mainmast to indicate that he had 'swept' the sea clear of English ships. A year later, after several English victories, Blake tied a whip to his own masthead to show that he had 'whipped' the enemy. Some historians now believe this story to be dubious – spoilsports! Blake died at sea off Plymouth in 1657. He was given a state funeral and buried in Westminster Abbey. However, after the Restoration, Charles II rather shamefully had his body disinterred and buried in a common grave near the abbey. There is a statue of Blake in the town centre at Bridgwater.

EXPLORER, NATURALIST ... AND PIRATE!

The explorer **William Dampier** was born in 1651 at East Coker. After a spell in the Royal Navy he joined the crew of a pirate vessel under the command of Bartholomew Sharp. During this time, their vessel circumnavigated the world, raiding Spanish possessions on the way. In 1688 he reached Australia, and was probably the first Englishman to set foot there. He wrote descriptions of all the plants and animals he saw on his voyages. In 1697 he published a book, *A New Voyage Round the World*, which became a bestseller. On the strength of this he re-joined the Navy and was given command of HMS *Roebuck*. He set off on a voyage of exploration, during the course of which his ship was wrecked, and the crew marooned for five years before being rescued. On their return to England, Dampier was court-martialled for cruelty, found guilty, and dismissed from the Navy.

Shortly afterwards he became a privateer, and set off on his second voyage around the world. It was on this voyage that a member of the expedition, a sailor named Alexander Selkirk, was marooned on the island of Juan Fernandez off the coast of Chile, where he remained for over four years before being rescued and brought back to Bristol. His story is believed to have been the inspiration for Daniel Defoe's novel *Robinson Crusoe*.

DEFENDER OF THE OCCULT

In 1662, at the age of 25, Joseph Glanvill was appointed vicar of Frome Selwood. A Devonian by birth and a Puritan by upbringing, he gained an MA from Oxford and was ordained priest in 1660. He was a keen student of philosophy and natural science, and promoted the idea that the best way of furthering our knowledge of the world was through experimentation.

Glanvill was disappointed by the tendency of the scientific world to dismiss the supernatural as mere superstition. He expressed his views in a book titled *Saducismus Triumphatus*, in which he supported the existence of witches and other supernatural powers and attacked those sceptics who did not believe in them (the 'Sadducees' of his title). The book contains a number of case studies examined by Glanvill and his friend, Robert Hunt. Glanvill later became rector of Bath Abbey and chaplain to Charles II. He died in Bath in 1680.

ROBERT HUNT – SOMERSET'S WITCHFINDER

Hunt was a Somerset magistrate and friend of Joseph Glanvill. Like Matthew Hopkins, the famous 'Witchfinder General', he set himself the task of hunting out witches in the south-west of England, particularly in his own county. One of his victims was Jane Brooks of Shepton Mallet, who was accused of practising her malicious arts on a 12-year-old boy, causing him to have fits (he was probably an epileptic). Witnesses were called and 'evidence' gathered that led to her conviction, and she was hanged at Chard Assizes in March 1658. Another unfortunate was Elizabeth Style, accused of causing the death of a local woman by her charms. She was also convicted, but escaped hanging by dying in prison in 1664.

THE KING'S ESCAPE

Charles II returned to England in 1650 in an attempt to regain the throne lost by his father the previous year. In September 1651 his forces met those of Oliver Cromwell's New Model Army at Worcester, where Charles suffered defeat. After the battle he escaped, and plans were set in motion for getting him safely away to France. What followed was a series of dramatic episodes and near misses, with Charles at one point famously hiding in an oak tree in Shropshire. After several changes of plan it was decided that he would travel to Abbot's Leigh in north Somerset, from where he hoped to be able to escape through the port of Bristol. Disguised as a servant, the king travelled with a small party to Abbot's Leigh, where they discovered that no ship would be leaving Bristol for France for at least a month.

It was therefore agreed that the party should head for the village of Trent, on the Somerset–Dorset border, and lodge with the Wyndham family, who were Royalist supporters. On the way they spent a night in Castle Cary. According to some accounts, they stayed at the Manor House, but local tradition says that it was in the nearby village of Ansford, where they would be far less likely to be discovered if a search was carried out. The following day they reached Trent, and twelve days later travelled to Shoreham, Sussex, where Charles took ship for France. It would be another nine years before he returned to England.

BLOOD ON THE MOORS: THE MONMOUTH REBELLION

When Charles II died in February 1685 he left no legitimate heirs, so the throne passed to his Catholic brother James, who ruled as James II. However, Charles had fathered a number of illegitimate children with a succession of mistresses, among whom was James Scott, Duke of Monmouth. He claimed that he was, in fact, legitimate, and was therefore the rightful king. He gathered a small army and landed at Lyme Regis, Dorset, in May 1685. He headed north into Somerset, recruiting more followers along the way. King James placed a bounty of £5,000 on his head, and sent a force under John Churchill and Lord Feversham to intercept Monmouth and his men, who by now numbered around 6,000. Monmouth entered Taunton to a rapturous welcome, then moved on with the intention of capturing Bristol.

The two forces finally clashed at Sedgemoor on 6 July, in what was to be the last true battle to be fought on English soil. Monmouth's troops, although enthusiastic, were poorly equipped and ill-trained; many of them were armed only with scythes and other agricultural implements, which is why this is sometimes referred to as the 'Pitchfork Rebellion'. They were outflanked and comprehensively defeated. Monmouth fled the field but was subsequently caught and taken to London, where he was executed on Tower Hill, where the job was botched. The headsman, Jack Ketch, was so inefficient that, after several blows, he had still failed to sever Monmouth's neck, and had to finish the job with a knife.

KIRKE AND HIS LAMBS

A name that has become associated with the Monmouth Rebellion for all the wrong reasons is that of Brigadier-General Percy Kirke (1646–91). He commanded the 1st Tangier Regiment, which was known as 'Kirke's Lambs' after the lamb emblem on the regimental badge. They fought for the King, and Kirke gained a fearsome reputation for his treatment of prisoners after the battle of Sedgemoor. Many were hanged without trial (according to some accounts, more than 100). He set up his headquarters at the White Hart inn at Taunton, and is said to have used the inn sign as a gallows. Kirke went on to become MP for West Looe, Cornwall, and a Groom of the Bedchamber to King William III.

HANGING JUDGE AND BLOODY ASSIZES

In the aftermath of the rebellion there was a campaign of vengeance against Monmouth's followers. The notoriously harsh judge, Lord Justice George Jeffreys, was appointed to carry out the reprisals and to preside over the trials, which became known as the 'Bloody Assizes'. Most of the victims were West Country men, many from Somerset. It is estimated that some 1,400 prisoners were dealt with, of which well over 300 were executed and 800–900 transported to the plantations of the West Indies. The Bishop of Bath and Wells, Thomas Ken, wrote to the King, saying: 'the whole air of Somersetshire is tainted with death'. Jeffreys was created Baron Jeffreys of Wem, Shropshire, and rose to the position of Lord Chancellor of England. When James II fled the country, Jeffreys attempted to follow him abroad, disguised as a sailor, but was captured in a public house in Wapping. He was imprisoned in the Tower of London for his own safety from the mob and he died there of kidney disease in 1689 at the age of 43.

BETRAYED BY MAN'S BEST FRIEND

One of the many casualties in the aftermath of the Battle of Sedgemoor was William Plumley, Esquire, who lived in the Manor of Locking near Weston-super-Mare. He had fought for Monmouth at Sedgemoor, but after the battle had escaped to his home. According to local tradition, when the King's men came calling he hid in a nearby tree (shades of Charles II), but unluckily for him his hiding place was given away by the excited barking of his dog, and he was arrested and subsequently hanged. An entry in the King's Warrant Book, dated 26 June 1688, refers to 'William Plomley, alias Plumbley, late attainted of high treason', and specifies how his property and possessions are to be disposed of.

A CHAMPION JUMPER

One rebel who had a lucky escape after Sedgemoor was
Somerset man Jan Swayne, of Shapwick, who was noted
locally for his athletic abilities. After being taken prisoner,
and suspecting he was to be hanged, he made a bet with
his captors that he could clear the Bussex Rhyne (a drainage channel) in a single jump. The soldiers didn't believe
it could be done, but agreed to let him try (stationing
two guards on the other side, just in case!). After a run-
up, Swayne's first huge leap easily cleared the rhyne. Two
more leaps sent the guards sprawling and took him into
the shelter of the woods, where he made good his escape.

THE DOONES – FACT OR FICTION?

During this period, according to long-held tradition, part
of west Somerset was being terrorised by a band of ruth-
less outlaws known as the Doones. They are said to have
been of noble Scottish birth, but were driven from their
own country and descended to the ways of plunder and
murder in the remote area around Exmoor. However, the
Doones are something of an enigma and they have been a
cause of much disagreement over the years.

In 1869, Richard Doddridge Blackmore (1825–1900)
published his famous novel *Lorna Doone – a Romance of
Exmoor*, which soon became a bestseller, and has never
been out of print. He had spent much of his childhood in
the area, where his grandfather was rector of the parish of
Oare, where much of the story is set. Using locations on
Exmoor itself, and sometimes involving actual historical
characters, it tells of a band of outlaws, the Doones, who
lived on the moor in the seventeenth century and terrorised

the neighbourhood, before being defeated and killed or driven out by the local population. A young girl, Lorna, kidnapped as a child by the Doones, is eventually rescued by the novel's hero, John Ridd, whom she then marries. The story is set against the background of the Monmouth Rebellion. A whole tourist industry has grown up around the book, and modern Ordnance Survey maps designate an area of the moor as 'Doone Country'.

But did Blackmore simply create the Doone legend for the purposes of his story? This has sometimes been suggested, but the answer is not so simple. Stories of the Doones were certainly known before the book appeared. In 1853 the vicar of Lynton had his collection of folk tales written out by the pupils of the local school, and they contained stories of the Doones, while the *Guide to Lynton* (1853) and the *North Devon Handbook* (1857) both contain sections on the Doones. Whether this band of outlaws actually existed or not, Blackmore certainly didn't invent them.

A 'BLOODLESS' REVOLUTION

After the Monmouth Rebellion had been put down, James II's popularity plummeted, partly due to his strong Catholic views and partly for his harsh treatment of the rebels. Eventually a group of senior government ministers sent to James's son-in-law, Prince William of the Dutch House of Orange, inviting him to come to England and take the throne. William arrived in Devon in November 1688 with a well-equipped army numbering around 20,000, and marched through Somerset on his way to London, gathering support along the way. He received the backing of many disenchanted local MPs, including those for Bridgwater, Taunton and Minehead. The last of these, Sir Francis Luttrell, even raised a regiment to help him. The MPs for Bath and Ilchester also came to his aid.

William's forces reached Wincanton a month later, and a group was sent ahead to reconnoitre the town. They found it defended by Irish troops loyal to King James. Although greatly outnumbered, William's scouts made a stand, and the Irish, thinking that the main body of the army was close behind, retreated. The death toll amounted to only about fifteen. William entered the town, but moved on the next day towards London. James then fled the country, leaving William and his wife, Mary, as joint rulers.

ONCE A REBEL, ALWAYS A REBEL

One of the most dissatisfied men in seventeenth-century Somerset must have been George Speke of Whitelackington, near Ilminster. He served as High Sheriff of Somerset in 1661 and, later, as MP for the county. In March 1683 he was part of an unsuccessful conspiracy to assassinate both Charles II and his brother James, Duke of York, in Hertfordshire, in what became known as the Rye House Plot. Despite searching his house for weapons, insufficient evidence was found to bring any charges against him.

Two years later he joined in Monmouth's ill-fated rebellion, which he survived (although his fourth son, Charles, was executed for his part in it). In 1688 George Speke joined the army of Prince William of Orange on its march to London, where William was subsequently crowned as William III. Speke died the following year.

BURIED IN WOOL

In the seventeenth century wool was still an important feature of the English economy, as it had been for centuries. It has been estimated that more than 100,000 sheep could have been grazing the hills of West Somerset in early Stuart times. However, the woollen industry was being threatened by cheap imports and by the introduction of other materials such as linen. In 1666 the first of several Acts of Parliament was passed, as mentioned in Chapter 3, stipulating that all bodies, except those of plague victims, had to be buried in a shroud made from pure English wool, on pain of a £5 fine. The parish register of Horsington, near Wincanton, has burial entries in 1678 for Mary, daughter of John Rawelins (28 October) and his wife Margaret (4 November), declaring that they were 'buried in woollen only'.

'RING OUT, WILD BELLS'

Many a Somerset church has a fine peal of bells, and a good number of them were cast by the famous Bilbie family of Chew Stoke. Founded by Edward Bilbie in the late 1600s, the company produced more than 1,300 bells, many of which still hang in churches all over the West Country. The earliest bell known to have been produced by Bilbie, and dating from 1698, is still doing its job in St Andrew's church, Chew Stoke. Other examples can be found in Axbridge, Keynsham, Glastonbury and Yeovil. Successive generations of the family continued bell-making until 1814, and they also gained a reputation as clockmakers.

THE PAPER IT'S WRITTEN ON

The seventeenth century saw the development of paper-making in Somerset (although the paper mill at Wookey Hole is known to have existed before 1610, and may be one of the earliest in the country). Prior to this, paper had been imported from the Continent, but, with the improvements in printing, the demand for paper became greater, and mills began to be set up in England. Paper-making needs plentiful supplies of fresh water from fast-flowing streams – something Somerset has in plenty. Many mills were set up in the county, particularly in the Mendip area, and for a time were successful. However, the development of steam power required larger and more elaborate factories, and so production moved to the larger cities where paper could be produced on a much larger scale.

The smaller mills were unable to compete economically, and most of the Somerset mills had gone by 1860. The one survivor today is, curiously enough, the Wookey Hole mill, which still produces paper on a small scale as a tourist attraction, using traditional methods.

6

GEORGIAN SOMERSET: ELEGANCE AND POVERTY

By the year 1700 the population of Somerset stood at around 228,000, when the total population of England was about 6.3 million. This put it about halfway down the table of counties in order of population size. It was still a predominantly agricultural county, with the majority of people living in villages, while the largest towns were Taunton and Bath.

BATH – THE GEORGIAN SPA

Ever since the Romans had first made use of the hot springs by creating their baths complex, there had been a small but steady stream of visitors coming to Bath in order to bathe in these waters in the hope of curing a variety of ailments. During the eighteenth century, however, the stream became a flood, with physicians recommending water-based health cures, and Bath rapidly became England's most fashionable resort for those in society. Handsome terraces, crescents and squares in the classical Palladian style were built in order to accommodate the influx of visitors arriving for the 'water cure'. The city also became a noted centre for gambling and other fashionable pastimes. Coming to Bath during 'the Season' (of which there were originally two: a winter and a summer season) became almost compulsory for the upper classes, with about six weeks being regarded as the minimum length for a proper stay in the city.

RICHARD NASH (1674–1761)

From humble Welsh beginnings, and through his charismatic personality and organisational ability, Richard Nash acquired in 1704 the position of Bath's Master of the Ceremonies, a post he held for more than fifty years. Known to all as 'Beau' Nash, he presided over Bath's social scene, formalising rules of dress and behaviour that all visitors, regardless of their social status, were required to follow. This provided a framework within which the whole of Bath 'society' could operate comfortably, with everyone knowing what was expected of visitors. Such was Nash's influence that his nickname of 'the King of Bath' was hardly an exaggeration. He was considered a wit, and many of his 'humorous sallies of wit, smart repartees and bons mots' were written down and published (although many of them might now seem quite tame to us). Oliver Goldsmith, who wrote a biography of Nash soon after the latter's death, records many of them, such as the occasion when a gentleman appeared on the dance floor in riding boots. Nash promptly asked him, in front of the company, if he had 'forgot his horse'. Nash was also Master of Ceremonies at Tunbridge Wells, and his codes of conduct, dress and deportment spread throughout the country. However, his fortunes declined steadily, and he eventually became poor. When he died aged 86 he was given a civic funeral in Bath.

THE TWO WOODS

Of the various architects whose work helped to create the Bath we know today, the most influential were undoubtedly the two John Woods, father and son. John Wood I (1704–54) was born near Bath but began his career in Yorkshire before returning to Bath with grand plans for developing the city in the Classical style. Although not all his plans came to fruition, he designed such masterpieces as Queen Square, the Parades and the Circus. He died, aged 50, while the Circus was still under construction, leaving it to be completed by his son.

John Wood II (1728-82) was born in the city and was trained by his father. After completing his father's Circus he went on to build the magnificent Royal Crescent and the Upper Assembly Rooms in Brock Street. He also worked outside Bath, designing such notable buildings as Buckland House, Oxfordshire and the General Infirmary in Salisbury, Wiltshire.

PLEASURE RESORT – OR SATAN'S THRONE?

A stay in Bath, apart from visiting the baths themselves to obtain relief from many ailments, would give you the opportunity to indulge in a variety of pastimes. Are you fond of dancing? There were three assembly rooms where you could attend a ball on most evenings, and learn the latest dances. Do you enjoy a gamble? Again, there were the assembly rooms, as well as a number of other gaming

houses in the town, with cards, roulette and other games
of chance, where fortunes could be won – and frequently
lost! What about a play? The theatre in Old Orchard Street
received a Royal Patent in 1768, enabling it to call itself the
Theatre Royal – the first such distinction outside of London.
Private parties, though discouraged by various Masters of
Ceremonies, were often held in the larger houses.

If you want to see who else is in town, go to the Pump
Room where, as well as drinking the waters, you can con-
sult the visitors' book. Then there are the Parades, where on
fine days you can saunter in your finery, and watch the other
visitors doing the same. And, if you have a son or daughter
of marriageable age, Bath is the place to come for match-
making. There are also the coffee houses, reading rooms,
and the chance to hire a horse or carriage to go sightseeing.

Not everyone, however, was enthusiastic about Georgian
Bath and its many attractions, and those of a more sancti-
monious turn of mind could be very scathing. The satirical
writer Ned Ward called it 'a Vale of Pleasure yet a Sink of
Iniquity', while the evangelist John Wesley referred to it as
'Satan's throne'. Strong words!

There were, of course, *two* Baths: the elegant and fashionable pleasure resort and the ordinary workaday Bath,
with its problems of overcrowding, poor sanitation and
poverty. Attempts were being made to alleviate the condition of the poor, and charitable institutions such as
St John's Hospital were doing their bit. The Mineral Water
Hospital was opened in 1738, thanks to the efforts of Beau
Nash, architect John Wood and local businessman Ralph
Allen, in order to provide free treatment for the 'deserv-
ing poor' who could not afford to pay. Wood designed the
hospital plans at no charge, while Allen donated the stone
and Nash persuaded wealthy visitors to part with some of
their money.

As a last resort for the desperate there was, of course, the parish workhouse; there were six of them in Bath in the 1770s. The largest, in Walcot, could accommodate 100 inmates. Beggars, pickpockets, prostitutes and other undesirables were very much in evidence in the lower parts of the town, such as Avon Street.

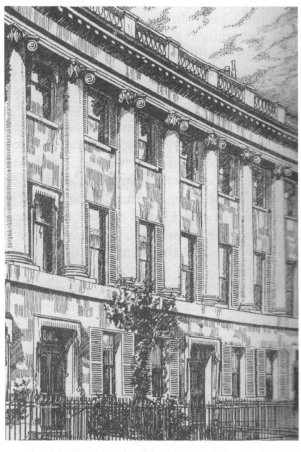

Royal Crescent, Bath

VOICES OF DISSENT

The eighteenth century saw an increase in the number of dissenting, or 'free', churches such as those of the Methodists and Baptists, and groups such as the Society of Friends, or Quakers. These found a ready acceptance, particularly among country folk and those at the lower end of the social scale, who responded to the message of those such as the Wesley brothers, founders of Methodism, who assured them that salvation was available to all, not just those with wealth or position. This led to friction between the dissenters and the established church, which saw Wesley and his ilk as a possible threat to the stability of society. Many members of the free churches were outspoken in their opposition to slavery, which made them extremely unpopular with those rich merchants who relied on the slave trade for their wealth. Efforts were made to disrupt meetings wherever possible. In Pensford, for example, at one of his open-air meetings, some opponents of John Wesley set an enraged bull on him. Even the great Beau Nash had a verbal tussle with Wesley when the latter came to Bath, but (unusually for him) Nash got the worst of the encounter.

The Society of Friends became established in Street in the mid-1700s, when several Quaker families came to prominence (of whom more later).

THE GREAT STORM

On 26 November 1703 the south of England was hit by an unprecedentedly violent storm. Thousands of trees were uprooted, roofs and chimneys torn off and ships sunk. Some estimates suggest that there may have been at least

9,000 deaths. Many, including the Church of England, regarded the storm as a sign of God's anger at people's sinfulness. Somerset was badly affected, with hundreds of people drowning on the Levels, together with huge numbers of livestock, due to the inundation of the sea. Records speak of one ship being found 15 miles inland! Whole orchards were destroyed, leading to fears of a cider shortage.

Among those unfortunates who perished from the effects of the storm was Richard Kidder, Bishop of Bath and Wells, who, with his wife, was asleep in bed in the Bishop's Palace when a chimney stack came crashing through the ceiling, killing them both. John Gill, churchwarden at Badgworth, near Axbridge, wrote: 'God grant that there may never be the like while the world lasteth.'

A NIGHT IN THE COOLER

Village lock-ups, sometimes known as round-houses or blind-houses, were a useful way of dealing with petty offenders during the eighteenth century, and several of these still exist in the county. These were small stone structures with a single door and a tiny window, where drunks and other disturbers of the peace could be held overnight, or until they had cooled off. Most lock-ups had a domed or pointed roof, and could be free-standing or attached to another building. A fine example of a round-house is the one at Castle Cary, and there is an octagonal one at Kingsbury Episcopi, near Yeovil. The Castle Cary lock-up was built in 1779 with money originally intended for the relief of the local poor.

DOWN WITH THE MACHINES!

Although the Industrial Revolution brought prosperity to many factory owners and businessmen, those lower down the social scale often suffered. New machinery meant that fewer people were needed to do the same amount of work, and the unemployed were often desperate to feed their families and to keep a roof over their heads. This led to widespread social unrest. In Shepton Mallet, for example, where there was a thriving cloth industry, there were riots in 1746, 1748 and 1749, with mills being attacked and burned. Frightened mill owners called on the local militia for help, and in the subsequent confrontations two of the rioters were killed.

Local mill owners became nervous about modernisation, and in any case were finding it hard to compete with the mills and factories in the north, and so the cloth industry declined. It was succeeded for a time by the manufacture of silk, but this did not last (although Shepton silk was used in Queen Victoria's wedding dress).

CANALS

The age of the great canal builders really started in the second half of the eighteenth century, and continued into the early part of the nineteenth. The first canals to be built

were the 'coal canals', used to transport this important com-
modity from the mines to the cities and ports of Britain.

A horse pulling a laden barge could move about fifty
times as much coal as it could if pulling a cartful, and with
many roads being in a poor state of repair anyway, the
choice was an obvious one.

The Somersetshire Coal Canal (as it was first called) was
begun in 1795, and engineered by William Jessop, together
with William Smith. Smith, who acquired the nickname of
'Strata Smith', was a geologist who pioneered the science
of stratigraphy, whereby the age of sedimentary rocks and
the fossils found in them can be identified by studying the
strata (layers) and how they overlie each other. He became
known as 'the Father of English Geology'. This narrow
canal had two branches, one from the Paulton coalfield
and one from Radstock. The two branches converged and
then connected with the much larger Kennet and Avon
Canal at Dundas, near Bath, a distance of some 10 miles.

The Kennet and Avon Canal was designed by the
great canal engineer John Rennie, and opened in 1810.
It connected the River Avon (which had been made navi-
gable between Bristol and Bath in 1727) with the River
Kennet at Newbury, then linked with the River Thames
at Reading. Goods could then be transported by canal
from Bristol to London, avoiding the longer, and poten-
tially more hazardous, sea route. Most of the cargoes
consisted of coal and stone, and by about 1830, 300,000
tons of freight were being carried annually. However, the
railways had already begun poaching some of the canal
trade, being far quicker. The journey by canal from Bath
to London could take a week; by rail it could be done in
a matter of hours. As more and more goods were sent by
rail, the days of canals, as commercial waterways, were
numbered. Many canals, including the Kennet and Avon,

were eventually bought up by the railway companies and fell into disuse.

TAMING THE LEVELS

The process of enclosing land, which had begun in Tudor times, did not have much effect on the moors of Somerset until the late eighteenth century. With the passing of the Inclosure Act of 1773, however, things began to change. Landowners could now enclose their land and displace the commoners who had previously had grazing rights on them. This was supposed to be done only with the approval of the majority of those affected, but the system was often abused, with landowners holding what were supposed to be public meetings in private. Between 1770 and 1830 the moors saw a dramatic degree of reclamation, with drainage ditches, or 'rhynes' as they are known locally, becoming a major feature of the landscape. Their banks were strengthened by the planting of willows, and new pastureland was created. The coming of steam power meant that powerful pumps could be built to deal with floodwater, and much more usable land became available.

GETTING AROUND

Eighteenth-century roads in Britain were a far cry from those we know today. Apart from the roads that had been laid out by the Romans (which were largely still maintained and were the best in the country), there were no main roads as we would recognise them. Most were little better than trackways; dry and dusty in summer and often impassable in winter. The roads that followed the higher ground were the least likely to be affected by flooding, and were therefore preferred (we still use the terms 'high road' and 'highway' today). Travel was, therefore, both difficult and dangerous, and not to be undertaken lightly. Daniel Defoe, in his work *A Tour thro' the Whole Island of Great Britain* (1724–26) complains that one of the two roads from Bridgwater to Bristol 'is not always passable, being subject to Floods and dangerous Inundations'. In Somerset the public roads were usually 40ft wide, with the central 12ft packed with stones to a depth of a foot in the middle and 9in at the edges, leaving a verge of about 14ft on each side.

Goods would be carried in wagons or on strings of packhorses, and there are still some fine examples of 'packhorse' bridges in Somerset, particularly those at Allerford, Dunster and Bruton. These bridges were built on recognised packhorse routes, are generally no more than 6ft wide and have low parapets either side so as not to impede the panniers the horses carried. There were also 'drove roads': wide, well-defined routes along which drovers could herd cattle, sheep or other livestock from place to place. A good example, which can still be walked, is near Crowcombe in the Quantock Hills. Another followed the route of part of the present-day A370 near Weston-super-Mare.

Human traffic, when not on foot, could travel locally in carriers' carts as they plied between the villages. Longer distances could be undertaken by stagecoach, the journey between Bath and London taking two days. Coaching inns were therefore important for the overnight comfort of passengers, some of whom would arrive half-frozen if travelling on top of the coach. These inns would usually have an inn-yard where the coach could disembark its passengers, and this would sometimes be reached through a '*porte-cochère*', an archway high and wide enough for a laden coach to pass through. These can be seen at the Royal York Hotel, Bath and the 'Talbot' inn at Frome.

The fastest coaches were, of course, the ones that carried the mail. They had the right of way and would travel through the night. The first high-speed mail coach ran from Bristol to London in 1784, taking just thirteen hours. There were two main postal routes from London through Somerset: one largely followed the route of the modern A38, from Bristol through Taunton to Exeter, while the other ran through Yeovil and Chard, along the route of today's A30.

STAND AND DELIVER!

As if travel by road was not already dangerous enough, there was always the unpleasant possibility of the coach being waylaid by a highwayman, or 'gentleman of the road', as they were sometimes (sarcastically) known. Although the penalty for highway robbery was death, this did not seem to deter these characters, who infested many of the more popular routes. Somerset was not immune from the attentions of these pests. Passengers on the way to fashionable resorts such as Bath could be expected to yield rich pickings. Farmers on their way home from market were also easy targets if travelling alone. Some highwaymen who operated in the county became notorious.

John Poulter

During the 1750s the area around Bath was terrorised by a gang of highway robbers led by a man named John Poulter. Coach after coach was held up, and passengers forced to hand over their valuables at pistol point. However, Poulter overreached himself when in 1753 he held up a coach and, when the passengers protested, threatened to shoot the child of one of them if they did not pay up. Unfortunately for Poulter, travelling on the coach was Dr Hancock, a local man. He was so angered by this display of callousness that he personally organised a hue and cry, with a large reward offered for Poulter's capture. This must have proved too tempting for one of Poulter's men, who betrayed him, and John Poulter was caught, tried and hanged from the gibbet on Claverton Down, near where the crime had taken place.

John Rann

Although he chose to operate around the London area, Rann was born near Bath, where, as a teenager, he served as a postilion to a local woman. Moving to London, he took up the occupation of highwayman, and was known as 'Sixteen String Jack' from his habit of wearing coloured strings attached to the knees of his breeches. His short career came to an end when he was publicly hanged at Tyburn in 1774 at the age of 24.

THE TURNPIKE TRUSTS

The setting up of Turnpike Trusts was the first serious effort since the collapse of the Roman Empire to provide and maintain a system of main roads in Britain. In Norman times the Lord of the Manor had seen to the repair of the roads, but that system was ineffective, as foreign wars were constantly straining resources. The Church also tried to do its bit, with some bishops offering indulgences for road repairs, but the Dissolution largely put paid to that patronage.

The Turnpike Trusts were local bodies, set up by various Acts of Parliament with the responsibility for maintaining the roads within their district, and empowering them to collect tolls for the purpose. The first of these had been set up at the beginning of the eighteenth century, and by the beginning of Victoria's reign in 1837 there were more than 1,000 of them throughout the country.

Tolls were levied on a scale, depending on whether the road user was, for example, on horseback, in a carriage, or driving animals. To ensure that these tolls were paid, gates would be set up at each end of a particular stretch

of road, and a toll-keeper employed to operate them and to collect the tolls. To discourage the more adventurous horsemen from jumping the gates, spikes (or 'pikes') would often be set into their tops – hence the name 'turnpike'. Somerset had many of these Turnpike Trusts. The Chard Trust, for example, was responsible for the maintenance of 45 miles of road in the area. The roads leading into Bath were among the first in England to be 'turnpiked' in 1707, and other trusts such as Bristol, Bridgwater and Taunton followed soon after. The toll gates themselves have disappeared, but some former turnpike cottages can still be seen in the county; the ones at Stanton Drew, Chard and Horsington are particularly fine examples. Many original turnpike milestones, show-ing distances to the nearest towns, have also survived at the roadsides. These were originally made of stone, and later of cast iron.

By their nature, Turnpike Trusts were open to abuse, and not all of the tolls collected would necessarily go into the repair of the roads. Like the canals, the system went into decline with the coming of the railways.

SMUGGLING

The eighteenth century saw the high point of smuggling activities in Britain. Increasingly punitive taxation by successive governments on imports such as wines and spirits, tobacco and silk meant that bringing these items into the country illegally could prove a very lucrative business. Even commodities such as tea were smuggled in order to avoid duties. In 1784 William Pitt the Younger, as Prime Minister, reduced the import duty on tea, when he calculated that, of 13 million pounds of tea imported into Britain, duty had been paid on less than half of them.

Many coastal areas of Britain became hotbeds of smuggling, and the West Country is particularly rich in secluded coves and beaches where contraband could be landed under cover of darkness. Records show that the trade was enthusiastically carried out along the north Somerset coast between Bristol and Porlock. Cargoes were brought in by the 'gentlemen' (as they were sometimes known) from France, Holland, Belgium and the Channel Islands. The ports of Watchet, Bridgwater, Minehead and Porlock were particularly involved with the landing of illicit cargoes, sometimes with the connivance of the port authorities and

local revenue officials, who would receive a cut of the profits. Sometimes whole communities would be involved in the racket. A number of secret hiding places have been discovered in and around Porlock, with false walls in cottages being a favourite ploy. Caves in the vicinity of Minehead, some only accessible at low tide, have long been associated with smuggling activities. St Martin's church at Worle had a hiding place for smuggled goods in the roof of the aisle, reached by a turret stair, while the island of Flat Holm in the Bristol Channel (once used for the isolation of cholera patients) has a cave in the east cliff that is still called the 'Smugglers' Hole'.

The punishments for being caught smuggling were harsh, and included execution by hanging, particularly for the leaders of the gangs. Contraband goods would often be publicly destroyed to try to convey the message that snuggling would not be tolerated, but the authorities must often have felt they were fighting a losing battle.

PARSON-HISTORIAN – JOHN COLLINSON (1757–93)

In 1791, the Reverend John Collinson, Oxford-educated and sometime vicar of the village of Long Ashton near Bristol, published his masterly three-volume edition of *The History and Antiquities of the County of Somerset,* in which he collaborated with his friend Edmund Rack, who carried out a survey of Bath. Like many clergy of his time, he was a keen antiquarian and seems to have had plenty of time to devote to his hobby. Although it received some severe criticism when published, it made Collinson's name and established for him a reputation as the county's foremost historian. This huge labour probably took its toll, however; he became seriously ill, and went for treatment to the Hotwells in Bristol, but died there at the age of 36.

AN AGRICULTURAL PIONEER – JOHN BILLINGSLEY (1747–1811)

Born in the Somerset village of Ashwick, where his father was a Presbyterian minister, he went into agriculture, farming about 4,000 acres (about 1,600ha). He became interested in improving farming methods, and was one of the founder members of the Bath and West Society (now the Royal Bath and West of England Society). In 1795 the Board of Agriculture asked him to carry out a survey into the state of agriculture in Somerset and in it he recommended many improvements, including ploughing with oxen using a double-furrow plough, enclosing fields with hedges, crop rotation and methods of treating sick animals. His suggestions were all geared to increasing the productivity of the land at a time when England and France were at war. He was also involved with canal building (being a shareholder and promoter of the Somerset Coal Canal), and in the setting up of Turnpike Trusts in the county. He died at his home in Ashwick, and there are memorials to him in St James's church in the village.

THE PRICE OF BREAD

The spring of 1801 saw Somerset affected by some of the worst food riots ever to occur in the south-west. The harvest of 1799 had been a particularly bad one, and the blockades caused by the French Wars led to an even greater scarcity of corn. Some people unjustly blamed farmers for hoarding their corn to inflate its value, and took to the streets to protest. The Home Office issued orders that such protests should be broken up using military force.

In March 1801 more than 100 people set out from Stogursey and by the time they reached Bridgwater their number had risen to about 1,000. They had a petition, which they presented to a Mr Noller, a Justice of the Peace. He reprimanded them and there was a scuffle in which Noller's coat was ripped and one of the protesters received a black eye. This was the only violence, even though the military were called out – they wisely declared their unwillingness to fire. Finally the protesters put their case to Mr Everard, another Justice, who promised to address their grievances, and, having received this assurance, they returned home.

Not all demonstrations ended so peacefully. The same year, two men named Tout and Westcott were hanged at Taunton's Stonegallows for their part in local disturbances.

THE PICKWICKS OF BATH

Eleazer Pickwick (1748–1837) became a prominent figure in the city of Bath. His grandfather, Moses, was a foundling who was rescued in the village of Pickwick, a few miles from Bath, and was named for the village. Eleazer started a coaching business in Bath based at the White Hart Inn, Stall Street (near the Pump Room), which was managed by Eleazer's nephew, another Moses. Both enterprises thrived, and the coaching business became one of the largest in the West of England, earning Eleazer a fortune. In 1795 he joined the board of the newly formed Somerset Coal Canal Company, into which he poured a considerable sum of money. He also invested in other local projects such as the Sydney Gardens Vauxhall, which opened in 1795. He owned a house in Queen Square, and bought Bathford Manor house in 1798. He became an alderman of Bath and was elected mayor in 1826.

It is generally accepted that Charles Dickens, while staying in Bath, noticed the name 'Pickwick' and decided he'd adopt it as the name of the main character in his debut novel *The Posthumous Papers of the Pickwick Club (The Pickwick Papers)* (1836).

HANNAH MORE (1745–1833)

Poet, playwright, philanthropist and social reformer Hannah More was born in Bristol, the daughter of a schoolmaster. At 22 she became engaged to a man named Turner, but after six years the engagement was broken off. Hannah suffered a nervous breakdown and went to recuperate near Weston-super-Mare. She received an annuity of £200 from her ex-fiancé, thus enabling her to pursue her own interests.

She spent some years in London, where she became acquainted with such prominent figures as Samuel Johnson and Edmund Burke. She wrote a number of plays and poems, and became a fervent abolitionist against the slave trade. In 1787 she bought a cottage in Somerset in the village of Cowslip Green, where she lived with one of her sisters. She began writing pamphlets and tracts on religious and ethical themes and carrying out philanthropic work in the Mendip area. She and her sister Martha were involved in the setting up of twelve schools, in villages such as Congresbury, Yatton and Wedmore, and did much to alleviate conditions among the local poor. In the district she gained the nickname of 'the bishop in skirts', and was unpopular among local farmers, who feared that educating the poor would be to the detriment of agriculture.

She died at the grand age of 88 and is buried in All Saints' church, Wrington.

ON THE TOURIST TRAIL

Towards the end of the eighteenth century, the outbreak of the French Revolution and subsequent war with France made travelling on the Continent a risky proposition for the English. It had long been the custom for wealthy young men to undertake the 'Grand Tour' of the cultural centres of Europe as a means of improving their education, and for those who could afford it to holiday abroad among the spectacular scenery of countries such as Austria, Italy and Switzerland. They now began to look for the picturesque a little nearer to home, and many found it along the northern coasts of the south-west of England. North Devon became popular, especially the rugged area around Lynton and Lynmouth, which gained the nickname of 'Little Switzerland', while Somerset has an area near Clevedon that is still known as 'Swiss Valley'. So Somerset also became a popular tourist destination, particularly among some of the so-called 'Romantic' poets such as Coleridge, Southey and Wordsworth, and also Tennyson. Three of these were to become Poets Laureate.

Let us meet them:

Samuel Taylor Coleridge (1772–1834)

Devonshire-born Coleridge became brother-in-law to fellow-poet Southey when they married the Fricker sisters in Bristol in 1795. Coleridge and his new wife, Sarah, spent the first months of their married life at a cottage in Old Church Road, Clevedon. The Coleridge marriage was not a happy one, however, and the couple were to spend much of their married life apart. In 1797 Coleridge rented a cottage in the Somerset village of Nether Stowey, and lived there for three years. During that time he produced some of his best work, including *The Rime of the Ancient Mariner* (1798) and the fragment *Kubla Khan,* inspired by an opium-induced dream, but said to have been incomplete due to being interrupted by the arrival of 'a Person from Porlock'. Coleridge Cottage is now in the care of the National Trust.

The poet's final years were spent in London, where he became increasingly dependent on drugs. He died in Highgate at the age of 61, and is buried in St Michael's church.

Robert Southey (1774–1843)

Southey was born in Bristol and educated at Westminster School, London (from which he was expelled), and then at Balliol College, Oxford. While there he made the acquaintance of Coleridge, who was visiting Oxford, and the two men became friends (and, subsequently, brothers-in-law). The two men collaborated in writing projects, and briefly experimented with setting up a commune in America. Although he lived for many years in the Lake District, Southey spent a good deal of time in Somerset. He and Coleridge began a walking tour of the county in 1794, taking in Bath, Cheddar, Bridgwater and Nether Stowey (to which Coleridge was later to return). In 1799 Southey took a walking holiday in the Exmoor region, visiting Minehead, Dunster and Porlock, where he stayed at the Ship Inn.

In 1813 he became Poet Laureate, a post he held until his death at Keswick, Cumbria, at the age of 68. In addition to poetry, he also wrote biographies and children's stories, the most famous being *The Story of the Three Bears* (1837).

William Wordsworth (1770–1850)

Born in Cockermouth in what is now Cumbria, Wordsworth published his first poem in 1787, the year in which he entered Cambridge University. More compositions soon followed. In 1795 he met Coleridge in Somerset, and the two poets became friends. Two years later, Wordsworth, together with his sister Dorothy, came to live in Alfoxton House, a few miles from Coleridge. The two men must have walked the route between their two homes many times. During their time here the Wordsworths were regarded by some locals with a degree of suspicion, due to their frequent walking (even at night), watching and recording. Could they possibly be spies for the French? One local doctor even wrote to the government to express his concerns. Nothing came of it, however, and the Wordsworths stayed at Alfoxton for a year, before moving to the Lake District.

Wordsworth succeeded Southey as Poet Laureate in 1843. He died of pleurisy at Rydal, Westmorland, at the age of 80.

Alfred, Lord Tennyson (1809–92)

Alfred Tennyson was born in Somersby, Lincolnshire, into a middle-class family. He attended Trinity College,

Cambridge, where he met Arthur Hallam, and the two men became close friends. Hallam's uncle was Captain Henry Elton, son of Sir Abraham, of Clevedon Court. Hallam was to marry Tennyson's sister, but tragically died in Vienna in 1833. His body was returned to England and interred in St Andrew's church in Clevedon. As a tribute to his late friend, Tennyson composed his famous poem *In Memoriam A.H.H.*, and in 1850 he visited Clevedon, staying in a cottage that is now known as Tennyson House.

On the death of Wordsworth, Tennyson was appointed Poet Laureate, and produced many memorable works, such as *The Charge of the Light Brigade.* In 1883 he joined the peerage as Baron Tennyson. He died in Sussex, aged 83, and is buried in Westminster Abbey.

THE FRENCH WARS

In 1793, following the French Revolution, Britain once more went to war with France. The threat of invasion by Napoleon Bonaparte's forces was constantly uppermost in people's minds. Counties with a coastline made preparations for resisting 'Boney' by creating and strengthening defences along the shore. In Somerset the Lord Lieutenant, Earl Poulett, formed the Somerset Fencible Cavalry in 1794, of which he was appointed colonel. Fencibles (from the word 'defencible') were regiments raised specifically to deal with the threat of invasion. The North Somerset Yeomanry was formed in 1798 as a cavalry regiment, charged, like the Fencibles, with the task of protecting the county in the event of an invasion. A second battalion of the 40th Regiment of Foot (also known as the Somersetshire Regiment) was formed at Taunton in 1799.

Even after Bonaparte's death in 1821, the threat of a French invasion did not disappear. In 1860 the British government, becoming concerned at the growing strength of the French navy, set up a Royal Commission that recommended strengthening coastal defences, including the building of a series of forts along the coasts. These were duly built, and were named 'Palmerston's Forts', after the British Prime Minister, Lord Palmerston, who had suggested the idea. One of these was built on the north Somerset coast in the 1860s at Brean Down, while gun batteries were constructed on the islands of Steep Holm and Flat Holm in the Bristol Channel.

THE IRON DUKE

In May 1814, the year before Waterloo, Lieutenant-General Sir Arthur Wellesley was created 1st Duke of Wellington. His many victories, especially during the Napoleonic Wars, are well known, culminating in the defeat of Napoleon's armies at Waterloo in 1815. When given the title of Viscount in 1809 he needed to choose a name to go with the title. Sir Arthur himself was still in Spain at the time, but his brother Richard discovered that the Manor of Wellington in Somerset was available, noted its similarity to the family name, and purchased it. Sir Arthur thus became Viscount Wellington, and, in 1814, Duke of Wellington. On a nearby hill stands the Wellington Monument, completed in 1854 as a tribute to the Duke's victory at Waterloo.

During the Napoleonic Wars many French prisoners of war were sent to Britain, and some found themselves in Somerset. Wincanton was one of fifty English towns that were used as bases for captured French officers, and was a temporary 'home' to about 350 of them. Once having given their parole, they were hardly treated like prisoners, but were allowed to wander freely in the town. They were even able to access their money from France, which they could then spend in the town.

THROUGH A GLASS

The glassmaking industry in Nailsea was started in 1788 by John Lucas, using the abundant supplies of local coal to fuel the furnaces. The company made window glass and also glass bottles, and by 1835 had become the fourth largest glass producers in the country. Nailsea glass was in great demand. In addition to the home market they also exported to America and the Caribbean. By the 1870s the industry was employing more than 300 people, but the dwindling supply of coal, due to the closure of some of the mines, eventually resulted in its closure in 1873. The site is now occupied by a supermarket.

7

VICTORIAN SOMERSET: GETTING THINGS MOVING

At the time of the first census in 1801 there were approximately 270,000 people living in Somerset, with slightly more females than males. The largest conurbation, the city of Bath, had a population of about 40,000. A large proportion of the county's inhabitants were still employed in agriculture, although considerable numbers were working in industries such as coal mining. Child labour was still common; for example, census records tell us that in 1851 there were two chimney sweeps between the ages of 5 and 9 years in Somerset. Figures for 1881 show that 8 per cent of the county's female population were employed as domestic servants.

The Industrial Revolution led to a decrease in cottage industries such as spinning and weaving, as these were gradually moving to factories in the towns. The population of Britain as a whole started to grow rapidly after the Napoleonic Wars, and agriculturists began looking at ways of increasing the amount of land available for food production. One way was by land reclamation, in which previously unusable land could be utilised, for example by drainage or clearing and then ploughing woodland.

The most notable change to agriculture in nineteenth-century Somerset took place with the sale by the Crown of Exmoor Forest to the Knight family. John Knight was a Worcestershire iron-master who, in 1818, paid £50,000 to acquire 10,000 acres (about 4,050ha) of Exmoor, subsequently increasing his holding to around 15,000 acres. He proceeded to build farms, construct roads, plant beech hedges and erect stone walls. He also put in measures for draining some of the wetland areas of the moor. When he eventually retired to Rome in 1842, the work was continued by his son, Frederic. He introduced new ploughing techniques and also imported Highland cattle and Cheviot sheep (along with their shepherds) from Scotland. At least one flock of Blackface sheep arrived at Temple Meads station in Bristol, and were then driven on foot (or hoof) the 80 miles to Simonsbath. Evidence of the Knights' improvements can still be seen at many places on the moor today.

CHILD MURDER AT RODE

The village of Rode was the scene of one of the most horrific murders of the nineteenth century. In June 1860, 16-year-old Constance Kent, of Road Hill House, was charged with the murder of her half-brother Francis, then almost 4 years old, whose body, with multiple stab wounds, was found in an outhouse. Although the boy's nursemaid had initially been arrested, Detective Inspector Jonathan 'Jack' Whicher of Scotland Yard was not convinced, and found evidence pointing to Constance as the murderess. She was arrested, but later released, the evidence being thought to be inconclusive. Five years later she confessed that she had in fact committed the crime out of jealousy. She was tried, convicted and sentenced to death, but this was commuted to life imprisonment, of which she served twenty years. On her release she emigrated to Australia, where she died in 1944 at the age of 100.

AN INDUSTRIOUS COUNTY

Glove making was an important industry in the town of Somerton in the early nineteenth century, and the town was also noted for the production of rope and twine. Yeovil, too, had a busy glove-making industry (its local football team is nicknamed the Glovers). Work in the glove factories would begin at eight in the morning and continue until ten at night. One of the small workrooms, run by a Mr Cleall, employed five girls, the youngest of whom was 8 years old. The children were paid from sixpence to one shilling per week. Pittards, the foremost manufacturer of gloves and leather goods in Yeovil, was established in 1826 and enjoys a worldwide reputation today.

Gypsum, an important mineral in the production of fertilizer, plaster and blackboard chalk, was mined at nearby Hurcott, using the open-cast system. Calamine mining in the Shipham area produced zinc for the brass foundries of Bristol, but these mines were worked out by the late 1800s. In the Mendip lead mines, improved smelting technology meant that further lead could be extracted from some of the slag heaps left by the Romans, and in 1865, 320 tons of lead were obtained from the Charterhouse workings in this way. However, this, too, came to an end at the beginning of the twentieth century.

Ironworking was an industry that was gradually moving from forge to factory, and the days of relying on the local blacksmith to make agricultural tools were beginning to fade. Companies such as Fussell's, which had premises in Mells, Nunney and Little Elm, were expanding their trade. The Reverend John Skinner of Camerton, writing in 1824, describes a visit to Fussell's to buy a new scythe, praising the tools they produced as 'the best in the county, perhaps in the kingdom'. He also notes the unpleasant conditions endured by the workers, and suggests that they would cause a public outcry if workers on the plantations in the Caribbean were forced to suffer them.

The movement known as the Religious Society of Friends, or Quakers, had grown in size since its mid-seventeenth century formation. Because in the early days its members were forbidden by law to enrol at university or to enter any of the professions, many went into business and were very successful; the names of some of the companies they founded are still well-known today (Cadbury, Fry's, and Barclays and Lloyds banks). A sizeable community of Quakers had settled in Street, and some started businesses in the town during the 1800s.

Most notable were the Clarks. Two brothers, Cyrus and James, started a sheepskin business in 1825 making rugs, and later expanded, very successfully, into the manufacture of slippers, boots and shoes. At the Great Exhibition in London in 1851 they won a gold medal for their galoshes. The Clarks were pioneers of technology, being the first company to mechanise the shoemaking process. This all came to an end in the 1990s and the redundant buildings were converted into the first factory outlet of its kind in the UK, Clark's Village.

A member of another Quaker family, John Morland, bought a tannery in Glastonbury in 1870, and founded a company that produced a wide range of sheepskin goods. This venture also enjoyed success, and during the Second

World War the company produced flying jackets and boots for the RAF. With the coming of the motor car it diversified into producing rugs, car coats and foot muffs for the comfort of drivers. Despite running into difficulties during the 1980s recession, the company is still in production, making shoes and gloves, although most of the original tannery buildings have been demolished.

A TRAVELLER'S VIEW

William Cobbett (1763–1835), politician, journalist and former soldier, travelled extensively through England on horseback during the early years of the nineteenth century. He kept a journal in which he recorded details and impressions of the towns he visited and the countryside through which he passed. His observations were published in 1830 in a book titled *Rural Rides*. In September 1826 he arrived at the Somerset town of Frome, which he described as 'a sort of little Manchester' with two or three hundred weavers at work. He also noticed large numbers of men, women and children working on the construction of a new road into the town, and records that their rate of pay was 2*s* 6*d* per week for a man, 2*s* for a woman, and 1*s* 3*d* for each child under 8 years of age (the average wage for a labourer at that time was between £12 and £20 per year). He also described the people of Frome as 'very intelligent'.

A FORTUNE FROM THE BIRDS

Tyntesfield, so named because it was once owned by a Tudor family named Tynte, is a Gothic revival house and estate near Wraxall, North Somerset. The property then passed through various hands, and in the early nineteenth century the then owner built a Georgian mansion on the site. The estate was bought in 1843 by William Gibbs (1790–1875), a businessman whose family had made a fortune from the importing of guano, or bird droppings, from Peru for use as an agricultural fertilizer. Gibbs was reputed to have become the wealthiest non-nobleman in the country. Although he and his wife lived mainly in London, frequent trips to Bristol and its port made it desirable for him to have a local residence. After purchasing the house and estate (then known as Tynte's Place) he renamed it and began a programme of rebuilding and enlarging the house. George Abraham Gibbs (1907–31) was created 1st Baron Wraxall in 1928, and the present holder of the title is the Hon. Antony Gibbs. The estate is now in the care of the National Trust.

ON THE LEVEL

Willow-growing on the Somerset Levels for the making of baskets has been going on for centuries, and was once a prime occupation there. By the end of the eighteenth century more than £6,000 worth was being harvested each year at the small hamlet of Stathe alone. The willows, or 'withies' as they are known in Somerset, are fast-growing trees that like a moist soil, and they are often found growing on the banks of streams and rivers. When grown, they are harvested and processed before being woven into baskets or hurdles, used for fencing. In 1819 Robert Coate, a willow grower and merchant, founded the company now known as P.H. Coate & Co., which still grows withies and makes baskets commercially near Taunton.

THE NOT-SO-GRAND CANAL

In 1796 an act of Parliament was passed that authorised the building of the Grand Western Canal. The idea was to construct a canal that would run from the River Exe in Devon to connect with the River Tone near Taunton, with various branches. It was intended largely for use in the transport of coal, lime and limestone. By the time work began in 1810 it had been decided that the canal should run only as far south as Tiverton, with an estimated cost of £220,000. However, the rise in the land along the route meant either the building of many locks, or else constructing lifts to raise the boats (which was the method finally adopted), at huge expense.

Sadly, the canal never repaid the shareholders' investment. By the 1860s the railway had reached Somerset, taking much of the trade, and the canal began to fail. The last section finally closed in 1924.

FULL STEAM AHEAD

The coming of the railway age brought about many changes in the county. Isambard Kingdom Brunel's Great Western Railway opened between London and Bristol in 1841 and, shortly after, trains were able to run from Paddington to Bridgwater. Other companies, such as the South Devon Railway and the Bristol and Exeter Railway, extended the routes further south-west, to Plymouth in Devon and Penzance in Cornwall. These trains originally ran on the Broad Gauge (7ft ¼in or 2.13m), which was the gauge Brunel had decided on as giving the smoothest and most comfortable ride.

However, other railway companies had settled on a narrower gauge of 4ft 8½in (1.43m), and many hundreds of miles of this track had already been laid out, making the two systems incompatible and necessitating the laying of expensive 'mixed' or 'dual gauge' tracks that incorporated both sizes. Eventually, Brunel was forced to concede, and the smaller gauge became the standard throughout the country. In 1851 the whole of the GWR was broad gauge; by 1891 that proportion had been reduced to about 17 per cent. Four years later the last of the broad-gauge track was replaced. Thus the 'gauge war', as it was known, came at last to an end.

This quick, convenient and relatively cheap means of transporting both goods and large numbers of people resulted in two things. First, commodities, especially bulk items, could be transported quickly from one location to another, which previously could only be done (much more slowly) by water. This resulted in the gradual decline of the canal companies, many of whom, as we have seen, were bought out by the railways. Second, it provided a huge boost to the tourist industry, with ever-increasing numbers of visitors coming to Somerset's seaside resorts, such as Weston-super-Mare, Clevedon and Minehead, and to the wide open spaces of Exmoor. Both of these factors helped with the growth of the county's economy.

Many of the smaller railway companies also played their part in the growth of the railway network in Somerset. The West Somerset Railway opened in 1862 and ran between Taunton and Watchet, originally on broad-gauge track, and twelve years later was extended to Minehead, a total of about 23 miles. It still runs today as an independent heritage railway, the longest of its kind in the country. An even smaller example was the West Somerset Mineral Railway, which carried iron ore from the Brendon Hills to Watchet harbour, for transport to the foundries of South Wales. Opened in 1854, it ran for a distance of only 11 miles. When mining activities ceased in the early 1880s the line survived, carrying passengers and small freight, until it finally closed in 1898.

CAN YOU HEAR ME?

In 1897, the Italian radio pioneer Guglielmo Marconi achieved the first wireless communication to be sent over open sea, when he successfully transmitted a message from Brean Down, near Weston-super-Mare, to Lavernock Point in South Wales, a distance of 10 miles (16km). The words of the message were: 'Are you ready?' Only four years later, Marconi was to send the first transatlantic wireless message over a distance of approximately 2,200 miles (3,500km), from Poldhu in Cornwall to St John's, Newfoundland.

TAKING TO THE AIR

In 1848, a pioneer of aeronautics named John Stringfellow (1799–1833) gave the first demonstration of his Aerial Steam Carriage, which he (perhaps unimaginatively) named *Ariel*. He was a former carriage builder from Sheffield and was fascinated by the idea of powered flight. He had experimented with an earlier model in 1842, but this had proved unsuccessful owing to the weight of the steam engine. Nonetheless, he patented it and six years later had more success with the improved version, which could fly a short distance. This represented a transition from gliding to powered flight, and so Chard, where these

experiments took place, often claims to be the birthplace
of powered flight.

BLACK GOLD

It is thought that coal was being extracted in Somerset even
in Roman times. The Roman scholar Solinus, writing of
Bath's Temple of Minerva in the third century AD, describes
the 'perpetual fire' that 'never whitens into ash', but, when
the flames die down, turns into 'rocky lumps' – a pretty
fair description of Somerset coal.

Coal continued to be extracted throughout the following centuries, but this was generally achieved by means of
a drift or adit (a horizontal shaft), or by digging 'bell pits',
fairly shallow holes that, like drifts, could only be used
when a coal seam was near the surface.

By the beginning of the nineteenth century, really serious mining was taking place. The Somerset coalfields were
employing around 4,000 people, and the coalfields covered
an area of about 240 square miles (62,000ha). The col-
liery at Farrington Gurney, which had opened in1782,
continued to produce coal until 1923, while the Radstock
collieries were being worked from pre-1790 until the
1950s. Much deeper seams were being mined; the deepest
shaft was at Nettlebridge, between Radstock and Shepton
Mallet, which reached a depth of 1,838ft (560m). Mining
became so intensive that, during the nineteenth century,
several pits closed owing to the coal seams having been
worked out. In 1872 the Somerset Miners' Association
was formed, eventually becoming part of the National
Union of Mineworkers. Kilmersdon, the last working col-
liery in the Somerset Coalfield, would finally close in 1973.
Today there is a very good museum in Radstock that tells

the story of Somerset coal mining. It has been estimated that there are still at least 11 million tons of coal remaining underground in Somerset.

Apart from being burned in domestic fireplaces, coal had many other uses. It was used to power steam-driven machinery, and from about the 1820s was used to produce gas for street lighting. It was burned in limekilns, which created lime for use on farms and in the building industry, and it was also heated to produce coke, used in the brewing and steel-making industries.

HARD CHEESE

Cheese had been made on Somerset farms for centuries, but the nineteenth century saw a marked growth in its manufacture. Some local farmers' wives began opening 'schools', where they taught the craft of cheese-making, greatly increasing the pool of skilled cheese-makers. Some of these took their skills to the newly emerging dairy processing firms such as St Ivel, which opened at Yeovil in 1901.

The cheese for which Somerset is most famous is, of course, Cheddar, which was being produced in the village as far back as the twelfth century. The rich pastureland supplied the milk, and the local limestone caves provided the ideal temperatures for storing and maturing the cheese. Originally, for cheese to be called 'Cheddar', it had to be manufactured within 30 miles of Wells Cathedral, but gradually the recipe spread worldwide, and today Cheddar cheese is manufactured as far afield as Canada and New Zealand.

In 1840 the farmers of West Pennard presented Queen Victoria with a cheese weighing more than 1,200lb to celebrate her wedding to Prince Albert. This monster cheese, believed to have been the biggest ever made, was more than 9ft round and took the milk of 730 cows to make! It was put on public display in London, but apparently Her Majesty refused to have it back afterwards, and it seems to have disappeared.

BESIDE THE SEASIDE

With the coming of the railways and improvements in road transport, it was possible for the ordinary family to get away on holiday into the country or to the seaside. This coincided with a growing enthusiasm for the health-giving properties of sea air and sea bathing. Coastal towns in Somerset began to enter on a new lease of life as holiday resorts, catering for an ever-increasing number of summer visitors; towns such as:

Weston-Super-Mare

This popular seaside resort began life as a small fishing village, which until the fourteenth century was known as Weston-juxta-Mare ('Weston beside the Sea'). The name was then changed by the Bishop of Bath and Wells, Ralph of Shrewsbury (whom we have already met). Until early in the nineteenth century Weston still consisted of only about thirty houses, but with the coming of the age of steam travel, many visitors began to arrive, either by railway (which arrived in 1841) from Bristol and the Midlands, or by paddle steamer from South Wales. The first hotel (the 'Royal') had been opened in 1810; many others now followed.

The medical profession began recommending Weston for convalescence and for those with bronchial conditions and similar ailments. In the late eighteenth century, doctors were also praising the health-giving benefits of sea bathing, popularised by George III and his visits to Weymouth. By 1900, Weston had become, after Bath, the largest town in Somerset, with a population of around 20,000. Two impressive piers were built: Birnbeck Pier (1867) and the Grand Pier (1904), and the town's future as a famous and popular seaside resort was assured.

Clevedon

Like its neighbour, Weston-super-Mare, Clevedon was originally a small village, though, in this case, an agricultural one. The name comes from 'cleave' or cleft, and 'dun' (a hill). The Domesday Book tells us that there were eighteen inhabitants and twenty-two cattle. The early 1300s saw the building of Clevedon Court, which excavations have suggested was erected on the site of a Roman building. In the 1600s the town had several watermills, including tucking or fulling mills. These were used for cleaning and thickening woollen cloth, using the local deposits of fuller's earth.

The increasing popularity of sea bathing, together with the picturesque local scenery, brought many visitors to the town in Victorian times. A stretch of the local coast path became known as 'Poets' Walk', due to the town's association with the Romantic poets mentioned earlier. Clevedon Pier was opened in 1869 to cater for the paddle steamers bringing passengers from Bristol, North Devon and Wales, with ironwork for the legs of the pier being reused from Brunel's South Wales Railway, whose rails were being replaced – a nice example of recycling. Salt water public baths were opened nearby. Salt for commercial and domestic use was also extracted from sea water, using large salt pans in the area known today as Salthouse Fields. Street lighting by gas was introduced into the town in 1864 by Sir Arthur Elton of Clevedon Court. Clevedon also has one of the oldest continuously running cinemas in the world: the Curzon opened in 1912.

Minehead

The name comes from the Celtic 'mynydd', meaning 'mountain', and refers to steep North Hill, which over-looks the town. In Domesday it is described as a manor belonging to William de Mohun (we met the Mohun family earlier). By the late fourteenth century Minehead had already become a small port, but it was not until the following century that it was improved by the addition of a jetty, thanks to a generous donation from the Luttrells of Dunster.

For many years the port traded in wool, coal, salt and other cargoes, but by the early 1600s the harbour had begun to silt up, resulting in the withdrawal of the town's charter by James I. A new harbour was constructed and trade improved for a while, with Minehead gaining trade from the decline of Porlock and Watchet, whose harbours were proving too small for the ever-increasing size of ships. By the nineteenth century, however, further problems with the port led to most of its trade being transferred to other, even larger, ports such as Bridgwater and Bristol.

The Victorian and Edwardian periods saw a great increase in the number of visitors to the town, which would grow to become Somerset's premier holiday resort.

SOME FAMOUS SOMERSET VICTORIANS

An Actor's Life

In 1838, John Henry Brodribb was born to a working-class family in the Somerset village of Keinton Mandeville. While working as a clerk for a London law firm in his teens he became fascinated by the theatre, and formed an ambition to go on the stage. He abandoned the office in order to concentrate on an acting career. His first appearance on stage was at a theatre in Sunderland, where he adopted the stage name of Henry Irving. He then moved to London and in 1871 his performance as Mathias in a play called *The Bells* earned him the praise of critics and public. He went on to gain huge fame as an actor–manager, playing many of the great Shakespearean roles at the Lyceum Theatre in the West End of London. His business manager at the theatre was the author Bram Stoker, and Irving is said to have been the inspiration for Stoker's most famous literary creation, Count Dracula.

In 1895 Irving became the first actor to be awarded a knighthood and he died in 1905 at the age of 67.

Two Somerset VCs

The first Somerset man to be awarded the Victoria Cross was a sailor with the delightful name of John Bythesea. Born in Freshford, near Bath, in 1827, he joined the Royal Navy in 1841, and was promoted to lieutenant eight years later. In 1854, while serving in HMS *Arrogant* during the Crimean War, he and a stoker named Johnstone captured important dispatches from the Czar, for which they were both awarded the VC.

In 1871, as a captain, he commanded the battleship HMS *Lord Clyde* in the Mediterranean, but unfortunately the ship ran aground, suffered considerable damage, and was never recommissioned. At the subsequent court-martial Bythesea and his navigating officer were severely reprimanded, and neither man was allowed to return to sea. Bythesea was not dismissed from the Navy, however, and was eventually allowed to retire with the rank of rear admiral. He died in 1906 and is buried in Bath Abbey.

In the churchyard of the Norman St John's church in Hatch Beauchamp you can see the grave of Colonel John Rouse Merriott Chard VC (1847–97). During the Anglo–Zulu War, while still a lieutenant in the Royal Engineers, he commanded the small garrison that defended Rorke's Drift in January 1879. This was a small mission station in Natal Colony, south-east Africa, which was attacked by 3,000 to 4,000 Zulu warriors, part of a force that had just defeated a much larger garrison at Isandlwana. The defenders of Rorke's Drift numbered about 150, and were mostly made up of soldiers of the 24th Warwickshire Regiment. Despite the huge odds, they managed to repel several attacks, and the Zulus eventually gave up and departed. Eleven Victoria Crosses (including Chard's) were awarded as a result of the action, together with four Distinguished Conduct Medals. Chard died at his brother's rectory in Hatch Beauchamp at the age of 49.

Education, Education …

Until the nineteenth century there was no national system of education, with only a small percentage of children receiving any kind of formal schooling. What there was existed mostly in towns, in the form of grammar schools and charity schools, set up either by generous benefactors or those who saw it as a way of making money.

The claim to fame of the village of Enmore, near Bridgwater, is that it was here that the first Free National School in England was opened. This was in 1810, and its sole teacher was the Rev. John Poole, M.A. Three years later he opened a similar school in Nether Stowey, its first teacher being a former pupil of the Enmore school. Both schools achieved a high reputation for the quality and diversity of their education.

'It's Fun to Stay at the YMCA'

Sir George Williams (1821–1905), the founder of the Young Men's Christian Association (YMCA) was born in the village of Dulverton to a farming family. Following an accident, he was sent to work at a draper's shop in Bridgwater. In 1841 he moved to London, where he again worked for a draper and was promoted to departmental manager.

Horrified by the condition of the London poor, particularly young working men, he and some of his fellow drapers combined to create a place where these young men could go in order to avoid straying and to occupy themselves usefully. This, founded in June 1844, became the YMCA, and provided a safe place for young men (and women) away from the streets. Williams would set aside two-thirds of the profits from his successful business to fund his work of charity. It developed into a worldwide organisation, which today has a membership of more than 60 million.

In the 1894 Birthday Honours List, Williams received a knighthood. After his death, aged 84, he was commemorated with a stained glass window in Westminster Abbey and is buried in St Paul's Cathedral.

A Spoonful of Sugar

Conrad Finzel (1793–1859) arrived in England at the age of 17 as a penniless German immigrant speaking no English, but went on to become the owner of one of the country's largest sugar refineries, in Bristol. In 1852 he had Clevedon Hall, which he originally called Frankfurt Hall, built on land that had once been part of the Clevedon Court estate. There is a small 'lookout tower' on Poets' Walk, built as a folly in 1835 by local timber merchant Ferdinand Beeston. Finzel is said to have used it to watch for his ships bringing home their cargoes of sugar from the Caribbean. He also apparently enjoyed a daily dip in the sea.

The Bristol refinery was burned down in 1846 and rebuilt at a cost of £250,000 (about £23 million today). After Finzel's death the refinery was kept going until 1881, when the business closed due to bankruptcy. In the 1940s Clevedon Hall became St Brandon's School for Girls; it is now an events venue.

John Skinner of Camerton

The Reverend John Skinner (1772–1839) was born in the village of Claverton, near Bath. After taking his degree at Oxford he worked in a lawyer's office in Lincoln's Inn, but soon decided to take Holy Orders and was ordained in 1799. In the following year he acquired the living of Camerton, where he remained until his death. He was a keen amateur archaeologist and antiquarian, and carried out excavations at sites such as Stoney Littleton and Priddy Nine Barrows. He travelled extensively through England and Wales and kept journals of his experiences. Life, however, was not kind to him; he lost his brother, his two sisters, and finally his wife, to illness, and seems to have become increasingly unpopular among his parishioners, who treated him badly. In October 1839 he walked into the woods near his home with a pistol and shot himself dead. He was 66. His *Journal of a Somerset Rector, 1803–1834* was published just over 100 years after his death.

William Holland (1746–1819)

A near contemporary of John Skinner, William Holland was a Welshman by birth, and became vicar of Over Stowey, near Bridgwater, in 1770. Throughout his time there he kept a diary in which he recorded the day-to-day happenings in the village, such as the birth of a calf or a plague of wasps. Occasionally he comments on news of national importance, such as his entry for Sunday, 24 October 1812, in which he records:

Not much in the newspaper except that the Russians are about to make Moscow very unpleasant Winter

Quarters for Buonaparte. I pray God it may turn out so, and that ... he may find his Grave in that place, and so rid the World of the Greatest Villain that ever appeared in it.

HELPING THE NEEDY

And what about the poor? They had always posed a problem for governments, who were continually trying to find practical ways of alleviating their condition. For a long time those in need had been the responsibility of the parish in which they lived, with money in the form of 'poor rates' being collected from householders. In 1834 the Poor Law Amendment Act was passed, which grouped parishes into larger units called 'unions' in an attempt to improve the efficiency of the system. Each union was administered by a board of guardians who were elected by the ratepayers. Large union workhouses were built (parish workhouses already existed, but they were much smaller). As an example, the Bath Poor Law Union was formed in 1836, and in the same year a new union workhouse was built, designed to house 600 people – even then, there were problems of overcrowding. The building is now part of St Martin's Hospital.

At the same time the Taunton Union was formed, together with the building of a union workhouse. They were not pleasant places. In 1849 an outbreak of cholera at the Taunton workhouse was blamed on overcrowding, bad ventilation and poor diet, but the guardians refused to accept any responsibility. In 1948 the building became Trinity Hospital.

GERMAN BEER IN SOMERSET

In 1872 the Anglo–Bavarian Brewery opened in Shepton Mallet, in the building formerly occupied by the Shepton Mallet Pale Ale Brewery. It used water supplied by the local water company because there was no natural source nearby. By 1889 the brewery, which produced a German-style beer, was lit by electricity provided by a steam engine-powered dynamo. The beer it produced was sold throughout the United Kingdom and abroad, overseas sales accounting for around 1.8 million bottles a year. During the First World War a drop in sales, probably largely due to anti-German feeling, resulted in the closing of the brewery in 1922, despite having dropped the word 'Bavarian' from its name. Trading began again on a smaller scale in 1935, but finally ceased with the outbreak of the Second World War in September 1939.

READ ALL ABOUT IT!

In 1860, Williton printer Samuel Cox decided to start a newspaper to serve the local community, and so the *West Somerset Free Press* was born. The editorship remained in the family for four generations, until the death of Samuel's great-grandson, Norman, in 1969. The company continues to operate under its current ownership, Tindle Newspapers, and maintains its traditional values as a family newspaper.

The *Somerset County Gazette* was founded in 1836, and is a weekly tabloid newspaper with a circulation of just over 11,000.

The *Bath Chronicle* began life in 1743 as the *Bath Journal*, and changed its name several times before becoming the *Bath Chronicle* in 1994. Originally published daily, it became a weekly newspaper in 2007.

CRICKET, LOVELY CRICKET

Cricket had been played in Somerset since the mid-1700s, evolving from the game of 'stow' or 'stob' ball. These were both local dialect words for 'stump', suggesting that the game was played using the stump or bole of a tree as the wicket. Somerset County Cricket Club was formed in 1875, following a game played at Sidmouth, Devon, between the Gentlemen of Somerset and the Gentlemen of Devon (which was won by Somerset). The club enjoyed only moderate success until the 1970s, when players such as Ian Botham, Viv Richards and Joel Garner helped turn Somerset into a trophy-winning side.

THE OVERLAND LAUNCH

At about 6.30 p.m. on the evening of 12 January 1899, the three-masted sailing ship *Forest Hall* sent out a distress signal. She was foundering off Porlock, in what was one of the severest storms ever to batter the Bristol Channel. Porlock having no lifeboat of its own, a message was sent to Lynmouth, just across the border in Devon, requesting their assistance. However, conditions made it impossible to launch the Lynmouth lifeboat from the harbour there, so the coxswain, Jack Crocombe, took the momentous decision to take the lifeboat to Porlock (a distance of about 13 miles), and launch from there. This was an almost superhuman task, involving taking the lifeboat up Countisbury Hill and down Porlock Hill – both hills having a gradient of 1 in 4.

Eighteen horses were employed to drag the lifeboat *Louisa* up Countisbury and across the moor. On the way, the crew and volunteers had to take down trees, walls and even the corner of a cottage, before reaching Porlock after a journey lasting more than ten hours. At one point the boat had to be removed from its carriage and dragged on skids to negotiate a narrow lane. They finally reached the wreck at about 7.30 p.m. the following day. Then, with the assistance of tugs, they were able to get the ship and her crew safely into Barry, South Wales, with no loss of life. Each crew member received £5 and a presentation watch – and a place in history!

SOMERSET'S BENEDICTINE COMMUNITY

In 1814 a community of Benedictine monks whose predecessors had been expelled from France during the Revolution, settled at Downside, near Shepton Mallet. A monastery was built here between 1873 and 1876, and in 1899 it was granted abbey status. Downside Abbey (its proper name is the Basilica of St Gregory the Great) is now the senior community of English Benedictines. The monks and lay staff also run Downside School, an independent Catholic boarding and day school that, in its modern form, opened in 1912. It became co-educational in 2004, and admits pupils aged from 11 to 18.

8

A NEW CENTURY: THE MARCH OF PROGRESS

The population of Somerset in 1901 stood at around 435,000. Some people still lived and worked in the countryside, but the towns were continuing to grow. Census records show that in 1951 only about 5 per cent of Somerset's population was employed in agriculture, whereas the figure 100 years earlier had been nearly 16 per cent. Bath's population was now approaching 50,000, while that of Taunton had exceeded 19,000 and Weston-super-Mare, 20,000.

A COUNCIL FOR THE COUNTY

Somerset County Council was established in 1889, when county councils were first introduced by an act of Parliament. It was responsible for the whole area of the traditional county with the exception of Bath. For administrative purposes Somerset was subdivided into a number of urban and rural district councils, and in 1894 parish councils were established, bringing local government into the hands of locally elected representatives for the first time. In 1974, under local government reorganisation, these would be amalgamated into larger district councils. In 2007 there was the suggestion that the county council and the district councils should be merged into a single unit, but this idea was rejected by a large majority when a referendum was held. Somerset County Council's headquarters is in Taunton.

DISASTER AT BREAN

At 5 o'clock on the morning of 4 July 1900 a terrific explosion ripped the heart out of the fort on Brean Down, which contained 5,000lb of gunpowder. The detonation could be heard as far away as Cardiff. Apparently the culprit was a certain Gunner Haines, who had been reprimanded by an officer. He was described as having a violent temper and in a fit of anger had fired his carbine into the magazine, causing the explosion. Ironically, the only fatality was Haines himself, whose head was blown off by the explosion. Shortly afterwards the fort was decommissioned and its guns were sold for scrap.

GHOSTLY GOINGS-ON AT GLASTONBURY

In 1907, shortly after reacquiring the ruins of Glastonbury Abbey, the Church of England appointed Frederick Bligh Bond (1864–1945) as official archaeologist. As well as being a scholar and architect, Bond also had a keen interest in psychical research. Within a few years, to the delight of his employers, he had found the remains of two previously undiscovered chapels, the Edgar and Loretto Chapels. Unknown to them, however, was the fact that he had gained the information of their whereabouts with the aid of his friend John Bartlett (also known as John Alleyne), a medium who had developed the facility of 'automatic writing'. This is a process in which the medium subconsciously produces writing by means of an outside agency, either of a spiritual or supernatural nature. Through this, the two men believed they were able to communicate with the spirits of two medieval monks, who directed them where to dig.

In 1919 Bond published his findings in a book called *The Gate of Remembrance*, which included full details of the psychic elements. At these revelations, the Church disowned both men and tried to discredit their work, and in 1922 Bond was sacked from his post, after which he emigrated to the USA, only returning to England in 1935. Today there is no reference to Bond in the visitor centre at the abbey, although the two chapels he discovered are there for all to see.

FRED WEATHERLY – SOMERSET SONGSMITH

Frederic Weatherly (1848–1929) was born in Portishead, the son of a doctor. In 1887 he qualified as a barrister, practising in London and then the West Country. He began writing songs that gained worldwide popularity, and his output was phenomenal. He is estimated to have written the lyrics to at least 3,000 songs. His works include such favourites as *Roses of Picardy, Danny Boy, The Green Hills o' Somerset, The Holy City, The Old Brigade* and *Up from Somerset*. He also wrote books and published several collections of verse. He lived for many years in Bath, where he died at the age of 80, and after a funeral in Bath Abbey was buried in Smallcombe Cemetery on the edge of the city.

'THE SEEDS OF LOVE'

In 1903 the composer and music teacher Cecil Sharp was visiting his friend Charles Marson, who was the vicar of Hambridge in south Somerset. While the two men were sitting in the vicarage garden, they heard the vicar's gardener, John England, singing an old Somerset folk song called *The Seeds of Love*. Intrigued, Sharp wrote down the words and the tune from the old man's singing. Realising that if these songs were not recorded they would disappear forever, he went on to collect many more such songs, which he published in book form as *Folk Songs from Somerset* between 1904 and 1909, and which led to his becoming one of the foremost collectors of traditional folk songs in Britain.

'WHERE THE CIDER APPLES GROW'

Thanks to its famous apple orchards, cider has been produced in Somerset for centuries, being made on local farms and consumed mainly by agricultural labourers and those working on the land (a part of their wages was often paid in cider). The locally made, rough cider is known in the West Country as 'scrumpy'. In 1924, however, after completing research at the National Fruit and Cider Institute at Long Ashton, a young man named Redvers Coate, a member of the withy-growing family mentioned earlier, had the idea of producing local cider on a commercial basis. His aim was to compete with the already established companies such as Bulmer and Whiteway and make Somerset cider known throughout the country. He began production in some empty barns, thanks to a loan from his father. Using his recently acquired knowledge, and only Somerset-produced apples, he began to produce cider of high quality, and was able to invest in up-to-date equipment, bottling his cider as well as selling it in barrels. Despite opposition from local breweries, the venture was successful and Coate's Cider achieved great popularity among cider drinkers and the public generally. On commercial television the jingle 'Coate's comes up from Zummerzet, where the cider apples grow' (a take-off of the Fred Weatherly song) became nationally famous.

In 1956 the company was acquired by Showering's of Shepton Mallet, which in turn was taken over by Allied Breweries in 1968. Today it is part of the Carlsberg Group.

'WASSAIL, WASSAIL'

Somerset is a county that maintains many old traditions, among which is the pagan ceremony of 'wassailing'. The word 'wassail' comes from the old Norse and Saxon tongues, and means 'be well', or 'be healthy'. The wassail ceremony, of which there are several in Somerset, is carried out in apple orchards, usually in January. The intention is to waken the trees and scare away any malicious spirits, thereby ensuring a good apple harvest later in the year. The date on which all this occurs is usually Twelfth Night (5 January), but in some villages, such as Carhampton, they do it on 17 January, the Old Twelfth Night (as it would have been before the reform of the calendar in 1752).

Those taking part make plenty of noise: beating drums, clashing pots and pans and even firing shotguns. Plenty of cider is consumed, and toast soaked in cider is hung on the branches of the trees. Sometimes mummers or morris dancers are in attendance.

BEVIN AND HIS BOYS

Ernest Bevin (1881–1951) was born in the Somerset village of Winsford. At the age of 11, after receiving very little formal education, he worked as a labourer before becoming a lorry driver in Bristol. He joined the local Socialist Society, becoming its secretary in 1910, and later a national organiser for the union. He also became a Baptist lay preacher, through which he developed his skills as an orator. Prime Minister David Lloyd George described him as 'a powerful fellow, with a bull neck and a huge voice ... a born leader'.

In the 1920s he became one of the founders of the Transport and General Workers' Union (TGWU). During the Second World War he was Minister of Labour in the coalition government, and after the war he became Foreign Secretary in the Labour government. He was involved in the creation of NATO and in the foundation of the State of Israel.

During the war years, with many coal miners having gone on active service, Bevin organised the conscription of young men between the ages of 18 and 25 to work in the coal mines in order to keep them functioning. These became known as the 'Bevin Boys', and numbered nearly 48,000. These lads were not always welcomed in the mining villages, as there were some locals who thought they were conscientious objectors (which they were not) or that they had come to 'steal miners' jobs'. Some were not released until several years after the end of the war.

'HOME IS WHERE ONE STARTS FROM'

The poet T(homas) S(tearns) Eliot was born to upper-class parents in St Louis, Missouri, in 1888, but moved to England in 1914 and later became a British subject. Learning that his family (the Elyots) had originally come from the Somerset village of East Coker, near Yeovil, he visited it in 1937, and in one of his works, *Four Quartets,* there is a poem entitled *East Coker,* which contains the words quoted above, and was inspired by the village. Eliot won the Nobel Prize in Literature in 1948, and died in Kensington, London, in 1965. His ashes, as he requested, are interred at St Michael and All Angels' church, East Coker.

A BAR OF CHOCOLATE

The two chocolate manufacturers J.S. Fry and Sons and Cadbury Brothers merged in 1919, and the decision was taken to move the former Bristol operations to a new greenfield site at Keynsham. This 228-acre (92ha) site was to be known as Somerdale, and to have full sports and social facilities, in keeping with the Quaker principles of the owners. This factory was eventually to employ more than 5,000 people, and produced a variety of famous brands such as Dairy Milk, Chocolate Cream, the world-famous Creme Eggs and Crunchie (which was produced at the rate of more than a million bars a day). The factory was acquired by Kraft Foods in 2010 and closed a year later, to the anger and dismay of locals, who had been promised that it would remain in operation. Production was moved to Poland, and the site has been redeveloped for housing.

OIL FROM THE CLIFFS

In the early 1920s there was great excitement in Somerset at the thought that the area near Kilve might become a major oil-producing centre. Geologists had identified large deposits of shale on the nearby cliffs, and exploratory boreholes had shown that the oil-bearing beds reached a depth of about 300m. A company called Shaline Ltd was formed in 1924, and the Kilve Oil Works began production. Things went well at first, with 700 barrels of oil being extracted in the first year. However, production costs proved to be much too high, and the operation was abandoned in 1925. A disused retort house and its accompanying shed can still be seen alongside the path leading to the coast.

MILLFIELD SCHOOL

Millfield school, near Street, was founded in 1935 by educationist and sportsman Rollo ('Jack') Meyer. He returned from India with seven Indian boys (six of whom were princes), and began the school in a large mansion that had once belonged to the Clark family of shoemaking fame. Four years later the school became co-educational, and gradually acquired more land and properties in the area.

Currently, about 75 per cent of the pupils are boarders, and apart from its high educational standards it is well known for its sports facilities, which include an Olympic-sized swimming pool and golf courses. The school has produced a number of international and Olympic athletes, including Mark Foster (swimming), Mary Bignal Rand (long jump) and Sir Gareth Edwards (rugby international). Former pupils are known as 'Old Millfieldians', or 'OMs'.

9

THE WINDS OF WAR

Britain declared war on Germany on 4 August 1914, and many of Somerset's young men were quick to enlist. The Somerset Light Infantry (SLI), which had been raised in 1685 as the Earl of Huntingdon's Regiment of Foot, was given the title of Prince Albert's Regiment in 1822 and became the Somerset Light Infantry in 1923. Across the whole of its career the SLI has gained five Victoria Crosses, three of which are now in the regimental museum in Taunton. During the First World War the regiment saw active service at Ypres, the Somme and Arras, and also in Palestine. Private Thomas Sage of the SLI was awarded the Victoria Cross for a gallant action near Ypres, Belgium, in 1917, in which he saved the lives of several of his comrades. They were sheltering in a shell hole when one of their number was shot in the act of throwing a bomb, which fell back into the hole. Pte Sage immediately threw himself on top of it, sustaining severe injuries. Another member of the SLI to achieve fame in later life was the actor and playwright Arnold Ridley, famous for his portrayal of Private Godfrey in the TV series *Dad's Army*. Born in Bath, he saw active service in both world wars, in the first of which he was badly wounded.

In the First World War the SLI alone suffered almost 5,000 casualties, and war memorials were erected in the towns and villages that had lost people in the conflict. Even the smallest villages and hamlets were involved. Only nine villages in the county lost no members at all, and these became known as 'Thankful Villages'. They are Aisholt, Chantry, Chelwood, Holywell Lake, Rodney Stoke, Shapwick, Stocklinch, Tellisford and Woolley. Two of these villages, Stocklinch and Woolley, were fortunate enough not to lose anyone in either of the world wars; these are known as 'Doubly Thankful' villages. Burrow Mump, the hill that rises above the village of Burrowbridge near Bridgwater, was presented to the National Trust in 1946 and serves as a memorial to the 11,281 Somerset servicemen and women who gave their lives during the two wars.

In 1915 the country's first Voluntary Aid Detachment (VAD) Amputee Hospital was opened in Chard, in the ballroom of Monmouth House. This hospital specialised in fitting amputees with artificial limbs that were specifically tailored to their individual needs.

Between the two wars, a major planning survey was undertaken, which looked at the ways in which areas such as agriculture, industry, roads and housing might develop in the coming years. However, these plans had to be shelved at the outbreak of the Second World War. Somerset became an evacuation area, with 10,336 children from London arriving at Weston-super-Mare station in September 1939.

In 1941, Weston-super-Mare's Birnbeck Pier was taken over by the Admiralty and became a secret weapons testing facility. Early testing of the famous 'bouncing bomb' designed by Dr Barnes Wallis, and used in the immortal 'Dam Busters' raid of May 1943, was carried out here.

In August 1940 the first German aircraft was shot down on to Somerset soil during the Battle of Britain. It was a Heinkel He 111 bomber, brought down by a Spitfire near Charterhouse. The five-man crew survived and were taken prisoner by men of the local Home Guard before being handed over to soldiers at nearby Yoxley Camp. A prime target for enemy attack was the Royal Ordnance Factory near Woolavington, which opened in 1941 for the development and manufacture of RDX, a high explosive.

On 28 October 1942 a B-24D Liberator, a long-range bomber of the U.S. Army Air Force, took off from Holmsley Airfield in the New Forest, on U-boat patrol. She carried a crew of twelve. On her return journey, at about 2.30 p.m., she encountered bad weather, and in poor visibility she clipped Bossington Hill and crashed on Porlock Marshes. Only one of her crew, Staff Sergeant H.E. Thorpe, a gunner, survived. There is a memorial near the spot where she crashed, which carries a small plaque made from the wreckage of the aircraft.

On 22 November 1945, another B-24 Liberator, this time belonging to the Royal Air Force, hit some trees on the Blackdown Hills near Buckland St Mary and crashed into a field, killing all twenty-seven people on board.

During the Second World War more than 400,000 prisoners of war were interned in camps throughout England, and many came to Somerset. Camps were set up near Wells, Wookey, Bridgwater and Norton Fitzwarren. Many of these PoWs were Italian and they were put to work on building and farm labouring. One such was Gaetano Celestra, who in civilian life had been a sculptor and mason. He was placed in Penleigh Camp near Wells, and worked for a local farmer. When a stone wall was damaged by a bomb, Celestra was given the task of repairing it and asked permission to erect a sculpture depicting two children being suckled by a she-wolf (the story of Romulus and Remus, legendary founders of Rome). The sculpture was completed and can still be seen by the side of the main A39 road.

DEFENDING THE NATION

In 1940, Britain was busy gearing up for a possible invasion attempt. There was constant fear of German invasion along our coasts, and Somerset, with its north-facing coastline, was no exception. At the western end of the coast were high cliffs, which made invasion unlikely, but on the lower-lying parts measures needed to be taken. Some beaches were protected with barbed wire, others with pillboxes such as the one at Porlock Weir built with pebbles to blend with the beach. Gun emplacements and searchlight batteries were set up at strategic points. The peninsula of Brean Down was rearmed with two 6in naval guns and a couple of searchlights. In 1942 the site was manned by the batteries of the Coast Regiment of the Royal Artillery. The site was also used for testing the 'bouncing bomb' mentioned earlier, as well as anti-submarine missiles. Other coastal batteries were set up to defend such beaches as Minehead, whose pleasure pier was demolished in order to accommodate the guns.

A line of defence was constructed that ran from Burnham-on-Sea across country to London, with another running south, roughly from Highbridge in the north to Axminster in the south. This one was known as the Taunton Stop Line. These defensive lines often followed the courses of rivers and other natural barriers, and were supplemented with pillboxes, tank traps, ditches and gun emplacements, designed to halt the advance of the enemy forces and contain them until reinforcements could arrive.

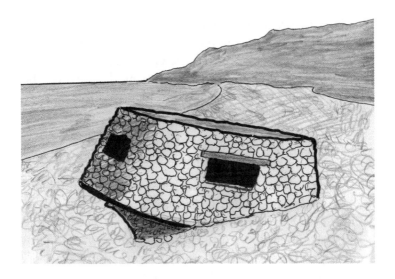

Many of the pillboxes can still be seen. Stop lines were often guarded by units of Local Defence Volunteers, or Home Guard as they became known.

In Somerset, one of the principal targets for enemy action was the Westland Aircraft Factory at Yeovil, which produced the Whirlwind fighter plane. When the factory at Southampton, which built Spitfires, was bombed in 1940, production of this aircraft was relocated to Yeovil.

To the north-east of the county, the city of Bristol was a prime target for enemy bombers because of its aircraft industry and the fact that it was also a major port. In an attempt to confuse the Luftwaffe, a 'decoy' city was built on Black Down Hill near Weston-super-Mare, constructed by film set builders from Shepperton Studios and modelled on Bristol. When the first wave of German bombers had gone through, fires would be lit to make it appear that the raid had been successful, and in the hope that the next wave would drop their bombs on the same target.

Despite this, Bristol suffered badly between late 1940 and early 1941, when, during the 'Bristol Blitz', it suffered six major bombing raids, during the course of which nearly 1,000 tons of high explosive bombs were dropped on the city and around 1,300 people were killed.

AIR DISASTER AT SCHOOL

On 15 May 1943 a cricket match between the school and the army was underway on the playing field at Downside School. Two Hawker Hurricane fighters began performing aerobatics at very low altitude over the field, when one of them clipped the tops of some nearby trees and crashed, killing the pilot and nine of the spectators and injuring fifteen others.

By a strange quirk of fate, in September 2013 a single-seater aircraft crashed in the grounds of the school, killing the pilot.

RAID ON DIEPPE

On 19 August 1942, 40 Commando was involved in a daring raid on the German-held port of Dieppe in France. They were acting in support of mainly Canadian forces in an attempt to destroy the coastal batteries that covered the principal landing beaches. They met strong resistance and 40 Commando endured many casualties, including its commanding officer, Lt Col J. Picton Phillips. The losses were claimed to be 'a necessary evil', but hardly any of the objectives had been achieved, and the event proved to be a victory for German propaganda.

THE BIG DIPPER

In 1941 more than 350 acres of farmland at Henstridge, near the Dorset border, were requisitioned for the construction of five runways. This took eighteen months, and when complete, the airfield became known as HMS Dipper, a facility on which young Royal Navy pilots of the Fleet Air Arm could practise deck landings on aircraft carriers.

During the Second World War several new hospitals were built in Somerset to cope with the large numbers of wounded who were returning from active service. One of these was Musgrove Park Hospital near Taunton, opened in 1942 as the American 67th General Hospital and staffed by the US Army Medical Corps. It became an NHS hospital in 1951.

10

MODERN SOMERSET: IN WITH THE NEW

Somerset today is still largely a rural county, with 42 per cent of people living in the countryside and 52 per cent in towns. Life expectancy in 2017 was 80.3 years for men and 84.1 years for women, with West Somerset having the highest percentage of people aged 65 and over in the UK. The main industry in the county is still farming, but tourism now comes a close second.

COME FLY WITH ME

In 1957 Bristol (Lulsgate) Airport was opened at Lulsgate Bottom in north Somerset. Built on the site of a former RAF airfield, it replaced Whitchurch Airport as the municipal airport for the area. Whitchurch was unable to extend its runway due to the proximity of housing, so the Lulsgate site was sold to Bristol Corporation for the development of a new airport. In its first year of operation it handled 33,000 passengers, and continued to expand over the next forty years. In 1997 its name was changed to Bristol International Airport, and by 2008 annual passenger numbers had reached 8 million. In 2010 a rebranding exercise took place, and the name reverted to Bristol Airport. It has become the ninth busiest airport in the United Kingdom, and at the time of writing is handling well over 8 million passengers a year and flies to more than 100 destinations. Currently there are plans for even further expansion to cope with the increased demand, with the aim of accommodating 12 million passengers a year.

GATEWAY TO THE WORLD

In 1978, facilities at the Port of Bristol were extended by the building of the Royal Portbury Dock, on the Somerset side of the mouth of the River Avon. Operated by the Bristol Port Company, it is a deep water dock with the largest entrance lock of any port in the UK. Its annual cargo tonnage is in excess of 12 million tonnes, and it is a major gateway for the importing of motor cars. It has excellent rail and motorway links, and is rapidly developing a role as a cruise ship terminal. Imported aviation fuel can be discharged straight into pipelines, which send it to major airports such as Heathrow and Gatwick.

THE TRAIN *NOT* STANDING ...

In 1963 Dr Richard Beeching. Chairman of British Railways, published his famous report *The Reshaping of British Railways* or, as it became known, The Beeching Report. Many of the smaller lines were losing money and Beeching's aim was to make the railway system profitable. As a result, more than 5,000 miles of track and more than 2,000 stations were closed.

In Somerset, lines such as the Cheddar Valley Line, the Norton Fitzwarren–Minehead Branch Line and the Bristol and North Somerset Railway were closed, and stations such as Midsomer Norton, Chard, Glastonbury and Burnham-on-Sea were decommissioned and sold off or left derelict. The Cheddar Valley Line was known locally as the Strawberry Line due to the high volume of locally grown strawberries it carried, destined for the markets of London and elsewhere. It was closed in 1963 and is now a popular route for walkers and cyclists.

AVON CALLING!

In 1972 the British government took the decision to rearrange the boundaries of many English counties for administrative purposes. In the West Country this involved taking a large area of north-east Somerset, plus some of south Gloucestershire, stitching it onto the city of Bristol, and calling the result 'the County of Avon'. This, people were told, would make for greater efficiency and better use of resources. This new creation came into existence on April Fools' Day 1974, a date that many local residents felt was appropriate. The move was met with a marked lack of enthusiasm from most people, especially those who felt a loyalty to the traditional county of their birth. Despite reassurances from the government that the changes were purely for administrative purposes, and that the traditional county boundaries would not be affected, organisations such as the Royal Mail and the map-makers of the Ordnance Survey began using the new 'county', and this crept into general use. One of the effects of this reorganisation was a notable decline in the population census figures for Somerset, which fell from 682,664 in 1971 to 417,457 in 1981.

Almost immediately following the creation of Avon, a 'Back to Somerset' movement began, and received widespread support. Dissatisfaction with this 'artificial' county persisted, and its creation proved to be much less successful than its enthusiasts had predicted. In 1996 Avon County was officially abolished, and the area split between four 'unitary authorities': Bath & North East Somerset, North Somerset, Bristol and South Gloucestershire. This move was generally met with two cheers, if not three. For a while it became a local joke to refer to the area of the former 'county' as 'CUBA' – the County that Used to Be Avon. The name 'Avon' is, however, still used in some cases (for example, the Avon and Somerset Constabulary).

In April 2019 two of Somerset's councils merged to become a single authority. Following government approval, West Somerset Council and Taunton Deane Borough Council will combine to form Somerset West and Taunton Council. The merger is expected to result in savings of more than £3 million a year.

A PLACE TO LIVE

In the 1950s Somerset County Council identified the need for a major house building programme for the county. This would mostly involve the development of smaller towns such as Weston-super-Mare and Clevedon, and has led to an enormous increase in the number of commuters travelling into the cities and larger towns, mainly by car. This naturally results in an increase in traffic congestion and pollution, problems which are of ever-increasing concern.

The network of motorways criss-crossing Britain was extended in the 1960s and '70s with the addition of the M5, which runs from its junction with the M6 at West

Bromwich to Exeter in Devon. On its way it passes through Somerset, from west of Bristol to just south of Wellington, a distance of about 50 miles. This motorway has become the main route to the south-west, with congestion being very heavy during the holiday months. For much of the way in Somerset it follows fairly closely the route of the A38.

A popular landmark on the M5, in a field near Bridgwater, is the Willow Man. This is a 40ft (12m) sculpture made from willows on a steel frame and shaped like a striding man, and was erected in 2000. Its locally based creator is Serena de la Hey. In 2001 the sculpture was the victim of an arson attack, but was rebuilt by the original sculptor with a surrounding moat to deter any future attacks.

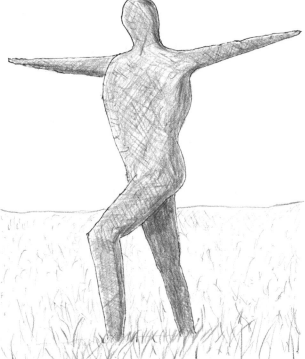

QUARRYING

Quarrying is an activity that has been carried out in the Mendip area for centuries, and the stone has been used in the building of many Somerset towns. Stone from the Doulting quarry was used in the building of Wells Cathedral and Glastonbury Abbey. Limestone was also crushed and burned for agricultural use, as it reduces the acidity of soil. Mendip quarries today produce 15 million tonnes of limestone per year, and provide employment for around 2,000 people. Much of the stone is used in the construction of roads; about 100,000 tonnes are needed to build just one mile of motorway.

However, quarrying is not without its controversy. Many local people are worried about the number of lorries that daily make their way through the sometimes narrow roads through villages. (When you consider that there are nearly 4,000 such journeys in and out of the area daily, they have a point.) Concern is also felt that, as the quarries become deeper, there is a greater risk of pollution of the water supply and possibly harmful effects on the water table itself.

BRIDGWATER'S 'BIG STINK'

For many years, anyone travelling through or near Bridgwater could not have been unaware of a powerful smell that seemed to permeate the area, and led to Bridgwater being nominated as 'Britain's smelliest town'. Many visitors must have asked themselves: 'What on earth is causing that?' as they closed their car windows. The answer was – British Cellophane. This company opened a factory at Bridgwater in 1937, and except for the war years (when it switched to producing munitions that included Bailey bridges), the 59-acre site manufactured cellophane, which it exported worldwide. The peculiar smell was an unfortunate by-product of the process. The development of alternative forms of packaging led to a drop in sales, and the factory closed in 2005.

KEEP THE WATER FLOWING

Providing sufficient water for the ever-growing population of Somerset is an ongoing problem. To cope with this, in 1905 the Bristol Waterworks Company created Blagdon Lake by damming the River Yeo to create a reservoir. This supplemented the much smaller Barrow Gurney Reservoirs, which had opened in 1852. However, by the 1950s these reservoirs were unable to cope with the increasing demand for water and a much larger reservoir was needed, leading to the creation of …

CHEW VALLEY LAKE

The reservoir known as Chew Valley Lake is the fifth largest artificial lake in the UK, with a capacity of around 4.5 billion gallons, getting its water from the nearby Mendip Hills. This reservoir supplies water to a large area of north Somerset, including much of Bristol. It was opened in April 1956 by the Queen, and has been designated a Site of Special Scientific Interest (SSSI). It is famous for the variety of its birdlife (more than 250 species) and is a popular centre for birdwatching. Before the area was flooded to create the reservoir, it consisted of good quality farming land, and a number of farms and houses were removed to make way for the lake. The land showed evidence of human occupation since Neolithic times.

GOOD MORNING, CAMPERS!

In May 1962 Butlin's Holiday Camp in Minehead opened its doors. William 'Billy' Butlin (1899–1980) was born in South Africa but came to England at the age of 7. He and his mother emigrated to Canada when he was 12, and he served in the Canadian Army during the First World War. He then returned to England, where he ran a fairground hoopla stall so successfully that he was able to start his own travelling fair and branch out into setting up amusement parks. He opened his first holiday camp at Skegness in 1936, based on the idea of providing accommodation, meals and entertainment all on one site. This proved so successful that he was able to open other holiday camps elsewhere in the country, and he became heavily engaged in charity work. He was given a knighthood in 1964, and died on Jersey at the age of 80.

The site for the Minehead camp was chosen because of its proximity to both town and sea and its transport links. It was extensively redeveloped in the 1980s, and now covers an area of about 165 acres (67ha), catering for both residents and day visitors. From 1987 to 1999 it was known as Somerwest World, before reverting to its former name.

In 1946 Fred (later Sir Frederick) Pontin opened a holiday camp on the site of a former US army base at Brean Sands near Weston-super-Mare. Pontin's camps were smaller and less expensive than those of Butlin's, and to entertain their visitors had Bluecoats instead of the famous Butlin Redcoats. Now known as 'holiday parks', there is another at nearby Sand Bay, which caters for adults only.

POWER TO THE PEOPLE

Construction began in 1957 on a nuclear power station at Hinkley Point, on the north Somerset coast near Bridgwater. The project was completed in 1965. The station, known as Hinkley Point A, had two Magnox reactors, cooled by the waters of the Severn Estuary, and producing 470 megawatts of electricity. These reactors were closed down in 2000, and the station decommissioned, but a second power station (Hinkley Point B) had begun production in 1976. This is powered by two Advanced Gas Cooled (AGC) reactors, supplying 965MW to the National Grid. This station is still operational and is expected to last until 2023.

In 2016 the government finally gave the go-ahead for the building of a new nuclear power station, Hinkley Point C, and its construction is currently under way. When completed, it will produce more than 3,000MW, using two Pressurised Water Reactors (PWRs). This would be sufficient to supply electricity to around 6 million homes. Projected building costs are in the region of £20 billion, and completion is due in 2025. Hinkley C is expected to have an operational life of about sixty years.

SPECIAL FORCES

In 1983 Norton Manor Camp at Norton Fitzwarren, just outside Taunton, became the home of 40 Commando, Royal Marines. The base provides a full range of accommodation, training and recreational facilities, and training is also carried out in the Blackdown and Quantock Hills and on the Somerset Levels.

Soldiers of 40 Commando served in France, Italy and the Aegean in the Second World War, and since then have been deployed in the Falklands, Northern Ireland, Iraq and Afghanistan. At the time of writing a decision has been taken to relocate 40 Commando from Taunton, probably to a site in Devon, in 2028.

'A-HUNTING WE WILL GO ...'

Fox hunting and stag hunting are activities that have been carried out in Somerset, and in particular on Exmoor, for centuries. Medieval kings hunted in the Royal Forest, and after Exmoor was disafforested (that is, no longer a royal preserve) it became popular with local landowners for the practice of bloodsports. This has always been a subject that has attracted fierce controversy, with some attacking it on the grounds of animal cruelty, while others defend it, stressing the damage done by foxes and deer and the fact that it is a long-lived tradition and way of life in the countryside.

Since the early twentieth century, attitudes have hardened, especially since the formation of the League Against Cruel Sports in 1924, and anti-hunting groups

have become more active. Clashes between hunt supporters and hunt saboteurs are a regular occurrence during the
hunting season. Over the years, several attempts to have
hunting banned by law were defeated. Finally, in 2004, the
Hunting Act was passed, which bans the hunting of wild
mammals with dogs. However, some claim that the activity still takes place under various guises, such as 'exercising
the hounds' or 'trail hunting' (following a scent-based
trail). So, whatever they call it, the sight of the local hunt
in full cry will probably still be seen on Exmoor and the
Quantock Hills for the foreseeable future.

WATER, WATER EVERYWHERE

On 10 July 1968 there was some of the worst flooding
the valley of the River Chew had ever seen, with Bath and
Keynsham being particularly badly affected. Following
an already wet summer, more than 5in of rain fell on the
region in less than twenty-four hours, turning the swollen
River Chew into a raging torrent that swept away trees,
bridges and cars, and causing damage to property that ran
into millions of pounds. The wall of water reached 10ft
high, with many people being rescued by boat, although
eight people lost their lives. In the aftermath, Army engineers were called in to erect Bailey bridges and help to
make damaged buildings safe.

A MUSICAL COUNTY

Somerset has produced its share of musical talent over
the years, and some names have become internationally known. We have already met Fred Weatherly from

Portishead. From the village of Pensford came Bernard Stanley Bilk (1929–2014), popularly known as 'Acker' Bilk (acker is a local word for mate/friend). A self-taught clarinettist, he formed his own band in 1951 and went on to achieve worldwide popularity, with such hits as *Stranger on the Shore*, the first single by a British artist to achieve the No. 1 spot in the American charts. The band were well known for their distinctive 'uniform' of bowler hats and waistcoats. Bilk was awarded the MBE in 2001.

The band known as The Wurzels was formed in 1966 by local singer/songwriter Alan John ('Adge') Cutler. Their comic style of music, sung with a strong Somerset accent and leaning heavily on local traditions of farming, cider and rural issues, became affectionately known as 'Scrumpy and Western'. They enjoyed great success, with their hit song *The Combine Harvester* reaching No. 1 in the British charts. Adge Cutler died in a road accident in 1974, but at the time of writing the Wurzels are still going strong.

GLASTONBURY – ENGLAND'S NEW AGE CAPITAL

During the late twentieth century, because of its Arthurian and other mystical associations, Glastonbury became a focus for New Age and Neo-pagan enthusiasts, and a sizeable community has sprung up within the town. An Order of Druids was established there in 1988, and in 2003 a pagan Glastonbury Goddess Temple was officially registered as a place of worship. Today, while walking around the town, it is quite common to encounter druids, hippies and people dressed as elves or goddesses.

GLASTONBURY FESTIVAL

The Glastonbury Festival has become an international phenomenon (although it isn't actually held in Glastonbury, but near the village of Pilton, some 6 miles from the town). Its origins can be said to date back to the early twentieth century, when, between 1914 and 1926, there was a series of concerts and lectures at a summer school in Glastonbury itself. These were known as the 'Glastonbury Festivals', and proved popular. In 1970 a local farmer, Michael Eavis, held a pop, blues and folk festival at Worthy Farm near Pilton, which attracted 1,500 people. Nowadays, apart from an occasional 'fallow year' when the land is allowed a rest, it has become an annual event, which has continued to grow year on year and now attracts crowds of more than 200,000 over a five-day period. It hosts internationally famous artists such as Lionel Richie, Beyoncé and Coldplay. In 2015 there was even an appearance by the Dalai Lama. Over the years the festival has raised millions of pounds for charity organisations.

CARNIVAL TIME

Each year, as part of the West Country Carnival Circuits, carnival processions are held in a number of Somerset towns. These celebrations are said to date back to the Gunpowder Plot of 1605, when the original carnival was held in Bridgwater, with the building of a huge bonfire and the burning of effigies of Guy Fawkes. Over the years the celebrations became more elaborate, with music, dressing up and a carnival procession.

Gradually, this spread to other Somerset towns, with the building of large carnival floats (or 'carts' as they are known in Somerset) becoming the highlight. Some of these can cost as much as £40,000 and take a whole year to build. Today the events are held in early November each year, beginning with Bridgwater, and several other towns such as Wells, Shepton Mallet and Glastonbury following. Another circuit, held in September, takes in such locations as Taunton, Chard and Ilminster. The purpose of these carnivals is to raise money for local charities.

GOING FOR GOLD

At the 1964 Summer Olympics, held in Tokyo, 24-year-old Mary Bignal Rand won a gold medal for the long jump, at the same time setting a new world record of 22ft 2¼ins (6.76m). She became the first British female athlete to win a gold medal for a track and field event, as well as the only one to win three medals in a single Games. The following year she was awarded the MBE. Rand was born in Wells, and on a pavement in the marketplace is a plaque depicting the distance she covered in her record-breaking jump.

OFF TO 'UNI'

Somerset has two public universities within its boundaries, providing higher education for thousands of students. Both are situated in or near the city of Bath.

In the 1960s a Bristol technical college needed to expand, and, with no space available in the city, relocated to Bath to become the University of Bath, receiving its Royal Charter in 1966. Today it occupies a high position in the university league tables, and its superb sporting facilities have enabled it to produce some top Olympic athletes such as Amy Williams, who won a gold medal in the 2010 Olympics in the skeleton bobsleigh event, and 2012 Summer Olympics rowing gold medallist Heather Stanning. The university currently has around 16,000 students, and notable alumni include former Lib Dem MP Don (now Baron) Foster and radio DJ and TV presenter Neil Fox. Its chancellor is HRH the Earl of Wessex.

Bath Spa University is mostly located to the west of the city at Newton St Loe. Formerly a teacher training college, it became successively a college of higher education and a university college, before finally achieving full university status in 2005. It has about 8,000 students, and famous alumni include Bodyshop founder Dame Anita Roddick, shoe designer Manolo Blahnik and cookery writer and presenter Mary Berry. The university's current chancellor is the actor Jeremy Irons.

SAVED FOR THE NATION

Under the National Parks and Access to the Countryside Act of 1949, the Quantock Hills were designated an Area of Outstanding Natural Beauty (AONB) in 1957, becoming the first area in England to be classed as such. The Mendip Hills followed in 1972. Under the same act, Exmoor became, in 1954, one of Britain's first national parks. The National Trust has acquired a substantial amount of land in the county, and now owns areas such as Brean Down, Cheddar Gorge and Selworthy Green, as well as properties such as Dunster Castle, Tyntesfield and Montacute House. Sites such as Cleeve and Muchelney Abbeys, Nunney Castle and the stone circles at Stanton Drew are in the care of the English Heritage Trust.

Since being designated as special areas, Exmoor and the Quantock and Mendip Hills have become increasingly popular with walkers and hikers, with many waymarked trails laid out and books of planned and graded walks produced.

MAKING A CONNECTION

In 1967 the tallest structure in south-west England was constructed on Pen Hill, near Wells. This is the Mendip Transmitter. Standing 961ft (293m) high and weighing in at around 500 tonnes, it broadcasts analogue and digital TV and radio over a wide area of the west, including Somerset, Gloucestershire and Wiltshire. It also handles telecommunications for mobile phone networks.

UP, UP AND AWAY

Since 1979 Ashton Court estate, to the west of Bristol, has been the home of the Bristol International Balloon Fiesta. This is an annual event at which teams of hot air balloonists from the United Kingdom and elsewhere in the world meet at the site to join in a mass ascent. It takes place in early August, and draws crowds of more than 100,000 to watch as many as 100 balloons ascending at the same time.

This event has come about as the result of the establishment of Cameron Balloons in Bristol. The company was founded in 1971 by Donald Cameron, an aeronautical engineer. The company is now the world's largest manufacturer of hot air balloons, producing around 500 a year. In 1999 a Breitling Orbiter balloon built by Cameron's achieved the first non-stop circumnavigation of the world by hot air balloon.

CRINKLY BOTTOM AND MR BLOBBY

On Saturday evenings in the 1990s many television viewers tuned in to *Noel's House Party*, a BBC light entertainment programme hosted by the popular presenter Noel Edmonds. He was assisted by a character called 'Mr Blobby', a grotesque pink figure covered in yellow spots. The series was filmed at Cricket St Thomas, near Chard, and in 1994 part of the grounds became a theme park based around the show. It was called 'Crinkly Bottom', and featured 'Mr Blobby's House', but closed after four years when the show came off the air.

Cricket St Thomas Manor (now a hotel) was also used as the location for the popular BBC series *To the Manor Born*, starring Penelope Keith, which ran from 1979 to 1981. From 1967 the grounds housed a wildlife park, but this closed in 2009 and all the animals were relocated.

THE FROME HOARD

In 2010 a hoard of more than 52,000 Roman coins, one of the largest ever discovered in Britain, was found by a metal detectorist near Frome. The coins, contained in a ceramic pot, have been dated from the period between AD 253 and AD 305. Some of the coins were minted during the rule of Marcus Aurelius Carausius (d. 293), the first Roman emperor to strike coins in Britain. They were valued at £320,250 and are now kept and displayed at the Museum of Somerset in Taunton.

CLEVEDON PIER

In October 1970, during stress testing for insurance pur-poses, two of Clevedon Pier's eight spans collapsed into the sea. The Victorian pier, described by former Poet Laureate Sir John Betjeman as 'the most beautiful pier in England' was now unusable. The district council applied for per-mission to demolish it, but this was refused and in 1972 the Clevedon Pier Preservation Society was formed. Local people campaigned to raise funds, and in 1984 grants were received from English Heritage and the National Heritage Memorial Fund that totalled £1 million. Some funds were also raised using 'sponsored planks'; donors could have their names inscribed on brass plaques attached to the deck planks. Work was finally completed in 1989, and the pier reopened. In 2001 it was given Grade 1 Listed status, and in 2019 celebrates its 150th birthday.

FROM BISHOP'S PALACE TO LAMBETH PALACE

In 1991 George Carey, Bishop of Bath and Wells, was appointed to the archbishopric of Canterbury, a posi-tion he occupied for eleven years. He was only the second person in history to move directly from Wells to become Archbishop of Canterbury, the first being John Stafford, who held the post from 1443 to 1452 during the reign of Henry VI.

SOMERSET AND THE EU

The EU Referendum of 2016, in which the public was asked to vote either to leave or to remain in the European

Union, split the county, with those in the south and west largely voting to leave, while those in the north and east wanted to remain. Overall, the majority of Somerset's voters were in favour of leaving, with the highest proportion of 'leave' voters (61.2 per cent) living in the Sedgemoor area, while those in the B&NES area voted 57.9 per cent to remain. The turnout for the county as a whole was just over 76 per cent.

WHAT NEXT FOR SOMERSET?

Somerset's history, as we have seen, has been a long and colourful one, with its share of ups and downs in peace and in war. Through all of this, however, it has been a resilient county, proud of its heritage and traditions, and will surely face whatever the future holds with its customary good humour and fortitude. The author Sir Compton Mackenzie once suggested that any county that has Bath, Wells, Glastonbury and Cheddar within its boundaries, even without anything else, is well endowed indeed. So the 'green hills of Somerset' will, no doubt, continue to welcome many thousands of visitors each year, eager to discover the history and delights of this very special part of England.

BIBLIOGRAPHY

Aston, M. and Burrow, I. (eds.), *The Archaeology of Somerset* (Somerset County Council, 1991). A useful summary by various experts of discoveries up to the 1500s.

Atthill, Robin, *Old Mendip* (Bran's Head, 1984). An in-depth study of a fascinating area of Somerset.

Barry, Jonathan, *Witchcraft and Demonology in South-West England, 1640–1789* (Palgrave Macmillan, 2012). Absorbing accounts of witchcraft trials and paranormal manifestations in the area.

Beisly, Philip, *The Northmarsh of Somerset* (Weston-super-Mare Heritage Centre, 1996). Very good general history of this often neglected area.

Burton, S.H., *The West Country* (Robert Hale, 1972). An excellent general account of the history, topography and folklore of the area, with much information about Somerset.

Byford, Enid, *Somerset Curiosities* (Dovecote Press, 1987). Well-chosen and well-illustrated guide to many of the county's unusual places, people and buildings.

Campbell, Elkington et al., *The Mendip Hills in Prehistoric and Roman Times* (Bristol Archaeological Research

Group, 1970). Brief but detailed account of discoveries in the area.

Collinson, John, *The History and Antiquities of the County of Somerset – 3 vols* (Bath, 1791). Exhaustive and thorough study by a former Somerset vicar.

Costen, M.D. *The Origins of Somerset* (Manchester University Press, 1992). Detailed study of the landscape and people up to the Norman period.

Down, C.G. & Warrington, A.J., *The History of the Somerset Coalfield* (Radstock Museum, 2005). A thorough and authoritative account of Somerset's coal-mining industry, with photographs.

Dunning, Robert, *A History of Somerset* (Phillimore, 1983). A masterly work by Somerset's leading historian.

Dunning, Robert, *Glastonbury: A History and Guide* (Alan Sutton Publishing, 1994). Excellent general history of the town.

Dunning, Robert, *A Somerset Miscellany* (Somerset Books, 2005). An absorbing collection of historical facts and stories from Somerset's colourful history.

Evans, Roger, *Somerset's Forgotten Heroes* (Dovecote Press, 2004). Very readable accounts of more than eighty exceptional men and women from the county.

Gibson, Alan & Gibson, Anthony, *West Country Treasury* (Ex Libris Press, 1989). A compendium of history, folklore and anecdotes about the area.

Holland, William, *Paupers and Pig Killers*. (Alan Sutton Publishing, 1995). Extracts from the diaries of a Somerset parson, 1799–1818. Fascinating account of daily life and doings in a Somerset village.

Hoskins, W.G., *The Making of the English Landscape*. (Book Club Associates, 1981). First published in 1955, often regarded as the 'Bible' for those interested in landscape history.

Jepps, Maria, *Wells: A History and Celebration* (Frith Book Company, 1994). Well written and beautifully illustrated portrait of England's smallest city.

Knight, F.A., *The Sea Board of Mendip: 1902* (Kessington Publishing, 2010). Comprehensive account of the history of Somerset's coastal region.

Little, Bryan, *Portrait of Somerset* (Robert Hale, 1983). A very readable and well-researched guide to the county.

May, Andrew, *Bloody British History: Somerset* (The History Press, 2012). Excellent and entertaining trip through Somerset's sometimes violent history.

Mee, Arthur, *The King's England* (Hodder & Stoughton, 1951). A village-by-village survey of pre-war Somerset, with lots of detail about its buildings.

Page, John Lloyd Warden, *An Exploration of Exmoor and the Hill Country of West Somerset* (Seeley & Co., 1890, reprint Bibliolife, 2009). A fascinating view of the area by someone who knew it intimately.

Page, William (ed.), *The Victoria County History of Somerset, Vols. 1 & 2* (Boydell & Brewer, 1906 & 1911). The 'Bible' for those writing about the history of the county.

Pearce, Susan M., *The Archaeology of South West Britain* (Collins, 1981). A scholarly description of prehistoric life in the area.

Pevsner, Nikolaus, *The Buildings of England: North Somerset & Bristol* (Penguin Books, 1958). Detailed architectural descriptions of all the significant buildings.

Robinson, Stephen, *Somerset Place Names* (Dovecote Press 1992). Fascinating and authoritative explanations of the origins of many of Somerset's place names.

Rutter, John, *Delineations of the North Western Division of the County of Somerset* (Longman, Rees and Co.,

London, 1829). A good general survey of the north-west of the county, with detailed information about individual towns and villages.

Skinner, John, *Journal of a Somerset Rector 1803–1834* (Kingsmead Press, 1971). A cleric's view of life and work in pre-Victorian Somerset, with fascinating detail about its people and customs.

Toulson, Shirley, *Somerset (with Bath and Bristol)* (Random House, 1995). A very accessible general history of the county.

Webster, C. & Mayberry, T., *The Archaeology of Somerset* (Somerset Books, 2007). An authoritative study, with many good illustrations.

Williams, Robin & Williams, Romey, *The Mendips* (Ex Libris Press, 1996). Very readable and informative, covering every aspect of this interesting area.

INDEX